Ludwig II

kleine bayerische biografien

edited by
Thomas Götz

MARCUS SPANGENBERG

Ludwig II

A Different Kind of King

For my parents
Martha and Siegmar Spangenberg

Verlag Friedrich Pustet
Regensburg

kleine bayerische biografien

Biographies bring the past to life: no other literary genre is able to connect human beings with their time, the particular with the general, the conditioned with its conditions in such a vivid way. With biographies, reading becomes both instructive and pleasurable. 100 pages are enough – enough to fill a weekend, a longer train journey, or two afternoons in your favourite café. But small does not have to mean lightweight: our authors are specialists able to render scholarly content easy to comprehend for readers who have a wide range of general knowledge but are not specialists on the topic in question.

Bavaria is well-nigh unique in its diversity: its great historical landscapes of Old Bavaria, Franconia and Swabia each have their own distinctive profile and many-layered history. They shaped the people who lived there – and were themselves shaped by the men and women this series is concerned with: rulers and scholars, politicians and artists, clergymen and entrepreneurs – and many more besides.

The aim of the Little Bavarian Biographies is to cast fresh light on well-known characters and (re-) discover lesser-known ones, opening them up for a discussion of contemporary regional identity in our increasingly globalised century. We believe this is a task with a future.

DR. THOMAS GÖTZ, the series editor, born in 1965, is a Lecturer in Modern History at the University of Regensburg. He has published on the city and its citizens in the modern era.

Contents

»My nature is simply different from that of most of my fellow men«

Preliminary remarks about a different kind of King

Ludwig II, King of Bavaria. Who was this 19th-century monarch, the subject of much speculation and many divided opinions? Today, in the 21st century, he is more famous than ever. The so-called »Fairy-tale King« has long served as a role model for artists, tourists, and drop-outs, who have been inspired by him and his creative endeavours –as has the advertising industry. Or maybe his eccentricity can help us to overcome the emptiness and lack of imagination of our present day and age?

The castles of Neuschwanstein, Linderhof and Herrenchiemsee are stone monuments to Ludwig II's failed life. They are hugely popular across the globe and are visited by more than two million tourists each year. The aim is to declare them World Cultural Heritage sites.

It is astonishing that even though more and more details about Ludwig's life and the underlying causes of his obsessive building are coming to light, the historical person, his aims, thoughts and creations, are rendered almost invisible in the wider public sphere by a fog of oft-repeated clichés and generalisations. This fails to do justice to a truly exceptional king and his ultimately tragic existence.

Ludwig II was not like other men, and he knew it: *»My nature is simply different from that of most of my fellow men,«* he acknowledged. He longed to be far away from the world *»that always denies me and which I will never, ever be able to or desire to befriend.«*

He responded to this world with an old-fashioned, religiously transfigured notion of kingship that he constantly – despite his supposed sins – strove to be worthy of. This fixation on the *»true, real«* royal office had precisely the opposite effect. The reality of the moderately powerful Bavarian state alienated Ludwig, and in 1886 he lost both his throne and his life.

The contrast between Ludwig's own claim to be a king by divine right and political necessity was widened by his inability to reconcile his poetic talent with the prose of everyday rule.

This book provides an account of the background, development and ultimately fatal consequences of this gap between dreams and reality.

»Hard is the task«

1 Ludwig II and the reality of kingship

On 12 March 1864, King Ludwig II of Bavaria noted in his diary, which he wrote in almost daily: »Saturday business, started at 8:30.« Then suddenly he appears to have turned the book around, writing »King!« right across the width of the page in huge letters.

Two days earlier, during the night of 9 March, King Maximilian II, Ludwig's father, had received the last sacraments in the royal *Residenz* in Munich. He asked for his son, who at this time was not even 19 years old. We have no record of what he had to say to him, but Ludwig left the room in which the third Bavarian King lay dying deeply shaken and in tears. Ever since his birth, he had been brought up to be his father's successor. A few hours later, around five in the morning, the mourning bell rang out over the Wittelsbach family's residence in the royal capital of Munich, announcing that Maximilian II had died after a short but serious illness.

Crown Prince Ludwig now became *»Ludwig II, by the grace of God King of Bavaria, Count Palatine of the Rhine, Duke of Bavaria, Franconia and Swabia, etc.«*, as his official titles called him. By the 19th century, the divine right expressed in these titles was more symbolic than possessed of any real significance. All the same, the 1818 constitutional charter of the Kingdom of Bavaria declared the monarch's person to be *»holy and inviolable.«* However, this did not protect the monarch against attacks on and restrictions of his power – nor did it protect Ludwig II.

Ludwig went pale and was evidently deeply moved when first addressed as »Your Majesty« by a servant at his father's deathbed. However, as his contemporary biographer Gottfried von Böhm reports, Ludwig quickly composed himself,

Ludwig II in the uniform of a general of the Bavarian army. – Photograph by Joseph Albert, 1864.

for *»the high and poetic ideals that he associated with kingship soon uplifted, delighted and intoxicated him.«*

Ludwig was familiar with the reality of being a Bavarian king. His father's reign had begun in 1848, when Ludwig, his first-born, was only three. His son thus knew what it meant to govern the most important middle power in Germany and to deal with the challenges and possibilities that a constitutional monarchy entailed. As yet, however, he had not been able to gain any real experience of ruling. At the beginning of his reign, his *»poetic ideals«* significantly outweighed his knowledge.

NAPOLEON CREATED THE KING

Bavaria owed its status as a kingdom to the self-proclaimed Emperor of the French, Napoleon I, who in 1806 raised his allies, the rulers of Baden, Bavaria, Württemberg and Saxony by one degree. Thus it was a revolutionary and social climber from the Corsican aristocracy, of all people, who turned the Electorate of Bavaria into a kingdom. Elector Max IV. Joseph became King Max I – and one of the freshly-crowned King's daughters was given to Napoleon as a bride for his stepson Eugène Beauharnais. This was the Bonaparte family's first link with an old aristocratic dynasty. The House of Wittelsbach had ruled Bavaria since 1180.

Ludwig's great-grandfather Max Joseph came from a branch of the Wittelsbach family from the Palatinate (the male line of the Bavarian side of the family had died out in 1777). Within two decades of his accession in 1799, not only had the entire structure of the state and the monarch's status within it changed – the very territory of Bavaria itself was altered. The final results of this development was a country whose borders have remained well-nigh unchanged to this day – with the exception of the Rhenish Palatinate (known as the »Circle of Rhine« up until 1835), which was given to Bavaria in 1816. However, with no direct land connection with the rest of Bavaria and strongly influenced by its time under French occupation, the Palatinate's position remained an exceptional one in many respects until it was incorporated into the new federal German state of Rhineland-Palatinate in 1946.

The young Kingdom of Bavaria gained several further territories, mainly in Franconia and Swabia. The years 1803, 1806, 1810 and 1816 mark the gradual emergence of a state whose parts differed significantly in terms of their culture, economy, social structure and religion. Accordingly, the role of the monarch as a figurehead unifying and integrating all of his subjects and all of the country's parts was an important one. The Bavarian kings sought to meet this challenge in different ways. For Ludwig II, it was to become one of his greatest problems.

On 1 January 1806 the Bavarian imperial herald rode through the streets of Munich, officially and ceremonially proclaiming the King and Kingdom of Bavaria to its citizens, and soon afterwards Bavaria joined the Confederation of the Rhine under Napoleon I. Nine years later, after Napoleon's defeat and the Congress of Vienna, Bavaria had become a member of the German Confederation and was thus an autonomous, independent and above all equal member of this association of Central European states. The Confederation collapsed during the reign of King Ludwig II in 1866. It was replaced in 1870/71 by the German Reich, into which Bavaria was integrated, losing its sovereignty.

Initially, Bavaria changed only little, remaining a predominantly rural and agricultural country, its landscape shaped by fields, meadows and vineyards. Farmers made up well over half of the population; around 70 percent of Bavarians were Roman Catholic, as was the ruling family. Coal and iron ore imports, which came mainly from Prussia, were needed to drive the beginnings of industrialisation. Overall, Bavaria was largely dependent on the major powers of Austria and Prussia and their politics in its attempts to shape its future.

THE TRUE RELATIONS OF POWER

Bavaria was a constitutional monarchy. The first Bavarian constitution was created in 1808, only to be replaced by another in 1818. Within this monarchy, Ludwig II as head of state united all sovereign powers in his person. At the same time, he was bound by the ministries of his own appointing, by parliament and – just like his subjects – by the constitution. Ludwig II was not an absolute monarch. This mundane contrast with his *»poetic ideals«* of kingship by divine right was heightened by the fact that in reality, the ministers determined policies, even though they were appointed by the King – and by him alone.

This gradual development had begun under Max I Joseph, who already accepted that his power was curtailed by his most important minister, Maximilian of Montgelas, who took over some of the King's tasks. While Max's son and successor Ludwig I was significantly more autocratic, he was unable to reverse the power relations, now constitutionally defined. The end of Ludwig I's reign during the 1848 March Revolution strengthened the Council of Ministers (made up of all ministers) still further.

The weight of the ministers' work was encouraged by Ludwig's son Maximilian II and his style of leadership. The ministers and officials increasingly understood themselves as the chief bearers of state power and saw their role as advisers to the King as of secondary importance only (even though the Constitution still defined them as such!). This was the situation in which Ludwig succeeded to his father's throne.

The main question was now how the King could use the power still available to him, and indeed whether he wanted to, and what strength and energy he was able to muster as head of state to control the events in his country and assert himself against the Council of Ministers if necessary. He was able to set state guidelines according to his own personal ideas. Laws only came into force after being signed by the King and countersigned by the co-responsible specialist minister.

However, the issue was who was to actively shape and define these laws. They were ultimately implemented by a bureaucracy that increasingly gained a momentum of its own, and this momentum had a key influence on effect of any regulation.

Despite the ministers' self-confidence, however, they remained dependent on the trust of the monarch who appointed and dismissed them. The parliament and its majorities played hardly any role in the appointment of ministers. Parliament was made up of two houses: the First House of imperial councillors (its members included royal princes, the highest officers of the Crown, the Archbishops of Munich-Freising and Bamberg, the President of the Protestant Supreme Consistory, the rulers of formerly self-governing principalities and counties and those appointed by the monarch) and the Second House of elected representatives. The latter exercised but little authority in Bavaria's constitutional monarchy. Their two most important rights were to set the budget and take part in the legislative procedure.

During his reign, Ludwig II appointed ministers exclusively from the liberal faction, even though they were in the minority in the Second House from 1869 onwards. Accordingly, Bavarian politics were determined by a liberal elite determined to preserve the structure of the state.

One institution held an important function that the constitution had not envisaged, at least not in the form it came to take. This was the Cabinet Secretariat, which served as an intermediary between king and government and thus played a key role. Under Ludwig II, its leader, who managed the King's personal affairs towards the public and was even able to influence political matters between the monarch and his ministers, was always a member of the liberal elite. This made it possible to cooperate smoothly with the ministers, something that was to become very important following Ludwig's withdrawal from his role as Bavarian head of state and unifying figurehead. The Cabinet Secretary was the only official who was able to see the King regularly and thus at least in principle had the opportunity to influence him.

The new King Ludwig II now had to act and perform his official duties within this complex system of government made up of monarch, ministry, cabinet secretary and parliament. For someone inexperienced in matters of government, there was nothing to be gained by *»poetic ideals«* – especially if history held in store tasks that would have posed a significant challenge to anyone in this position. Even though he knew nothing of this at the time of his accession in March 1864, Ludwig declared: *»Great and heavy is the task appointed to me.«* He continued: *»I rely on God to send me the light and the strength I require to fulfil it.«*

KINGSHIP BY DIVINE RIGHT

The continuing influence of the image of the ruler by divine right was hardly compatible with these changing times. Nevertheless, this concept was to have a greater influence on Ludwig II than on any of his predecessors. Such was the significance he accorded to the conferment of the royal office by God – not by strength of arms or any individual achievement – that he believed the king owed responsibility to God alone. The monarch's legitimation by God meant he had a duty to act in a manner informed by a Christian ethos. Ludwig's father, King Maximilian II, was already told at his First Communion to become a ruler *»enlightened by the Spirit of Christ, inflamed by the love of Christ, strengthened by the Word of Christ, guided by Christ's mercy towards his people...an image of the eternal God.«* This was part of the long family tradition of princely education. It had already been stated many decades previously that a ruler must *»show through [his] contempt for every lesser sin that [he] prizes God and [his] salvation more highly than all the pleasures of the flesh...more highly than life itself.«*

Ludwig II, King of Bavaria, was to prove that it was possible to exaggerate this attitude even further; taken together with his problems of an expressly personal nature, the notion of divine right was to develop into a disastrous understanding of kingship. Ludwig saw himself as a Christian knight whose duty it was to serve as an intermediary between God and people, remaining exemplary and free of sin in doing so.

»How quickly these 18 years have passed«

2 Childhood and boyhood influences

Maximilian had searched for a bride for such a long time that his father, King Ludwig I, jokingly called his son the *»footsore suitor«*. The Crown Prince paid his respects to many marriageable German princesses of the same rank as himself who were keen to enter into wedlock. Finally, after having gained her family's approval, 31-year-old Maximilian ventured to propose to a niece of the Prussian King, Princess Marie Friederike of Prussia, who was not even 17 years old at the time. *»The greatest jewel among women, the fair queen of roses is now found,«* the happy bridegroom wrote in his future wife's album of verses.

As the Hohenzollern family was Protestant, there were two separate weddings. The first wedding – according to Protestant rite – took place on 5 October 1842 in the chapel of the Berlin City Palace. The Catholic bridegroom was not present; the bride's cousin, the future King of Prussia and German Emperor Wilhelm I, acted as his proxy. The actual wedding was the second one, which followed a week later at the Court Church of All Saints in Munich.

Tens of thousands of onlookers gathered under the blue Bavarian skies to view the spectacle of the royal wedding. After all, Maximilian's father Ludwig had married his wife Therese (also a Protestant) on the same day 32 years previously – thus founding the *Oktoberfest*, which has been celebrated annually ever since.

On 12 October 1842, the *Gebirgsschützen* – traditional Bavarian rifle clubs – and musicians set the scene. *»What a promising future!«* enthused the philosopher Friedrich Wilhelm von Schelling. The wedding marked the union of two prominent and politically important German dynasties, and the marriage was expected to produce male offspring that would continue the main Wittelsbach line.

Ludwig with his parents, Queen Marie and King Maximilian II of Bavaria, and his brother Otto (right). – Photograph, 1861.

»MARIE WAS DELIVERED OF A SON«

In the early hours of 24 August 1845, Marie went into labour at Nymphenburg Palace, the Wittelsbach summer residence near Munich. The future parents were not the only ones to celebrate: King Ludwig I, accompanied by his wife Therese, rushed to Nymphenburg in order to witness the birth. The older Ludwig was hoping that the child would be born not on 24 August, but on the next day, 25 August, which was his own birthday and name day. The baby arrived just after midnight, and its grandfather's wish was granted: »*At twenty minutes past the hour by the Nymphenburg clock, at thirty minutes by my own watch (and thus in the same hour that I myself was born 59 years ago) Marie was delivered of a son,*« Ludwig I noted proudly. The time of birth noted by the King on 25 August was declared the official time of birth. For the first days of his life, the newborn prince was called Otto. However, following the promptings of the baby's grandfather Ludwig, who pointed out that his grandson had been born on the feast day of

St Louis IX of France, Max and Marie decided the boy's principal name would be Ludwig.

In the first months of his life, Ludwig gave his parents Max and Marie great pleasure. In November 1845, his mother wrote: »*Our little son is as healthy as can be, he laughs a lot and is very lively.*« However, Ludwig's cheerfulness and liveliness were dampened considerably towards the end of March 1846, when his wet nurse, a country woman from Miesbach, fell ill; she died soon after, most likely of meningitis. The infant had to be weaned immediately. While the family's personal doctor Franz Xaver von Gietl stated on 15 April 1846 that the boy was so strong »*...that this sudden weaning, necessitated by the wet nurse's fever, had no effect on his health...*«, little Ludwig was soon afterwards affected by such strong cramps and attacks of fever that there was great concern for his health. At the time, Marie and her husband were in Berlin visiting her mother, who was seriously ill and died in mid-April. Following this sad event, Marie's longing for her son increased greatly, but Ludwig I forbade his weakened grandson to travel. Marie did not see her son again until June. In the meantime he had regained his health, but only after many weeks of sickness. »*A slight pallor is likely to be the only lasting effect of the fever, which the heir has now almost completely overcome,*« the court physician stated reassuringly in July 1846. Many modern psychologists and psychiatrists now doubt whether he was right. This early loss of the person closest to him (it was usual for royal babies not to be breastfed by their own mothers) and possible transmission of germs by the wet nurse are often cited as a possible explanation for Ludwig II's later behaviour.

TURNING POINT

The year 1848 began happily for Marie, who became pregnant for the second time. However, the political situation in Munich was growing increasingly tense. Nearly every country in Europe was gripped by the spirit of revolution. The situation in Bavaria was exacerbated by Ludwig I's autocratic attitude and his affair with the Irish dancer Lola Montez. Following the French Revolution and the proclamation of the Second French Republic, demands for greater participation in government gained ever greater popular support. On 6 March, bowing to pressure from the streets, King Ludwig I proclaimed his acceptance of key civic demands: *»Gather around the throne. United with Your ruler, represented by Your constitutional institutions, let Us consider what We and what Our common Fatherland needs.«* This did indeed calm the situation somewhat at first. However, the royal family had not given in out of conviction, but because they were afraid of losing the crown. On 16 March, there were fresh riots following rumours about Lola Montez, who was hated passionately by the Bavarian people.

On 20 March, Ludwig I was forced to abdicate in favour of his son Maximilian. Initially, Maximilian was greeted with little enthusiasm by the populace, for he had not been a very popular Crown Prince. Their scepticism seemed well justified. Although Maximilian publicly declared *»I am proud to call myself a constitutional monarch«* in his King's speech, he certainly had no enthusiasm for the reforms demanded. However, he was forced to give in, although he defended his royal privileges fiercely. It is thus hardly surprising that a few years later, Maximilian II introduced harsh repressions of the press, associations and assemblies in an attempt to suppress any liberal or democratic tendencies amongst the population. As he gained in confidence, Ludwig II's father sought to consolidate his royal privileges.

All that remained of the revolution was the universal, indirect suffrage with electors (instead of the previous estate-based electoral system), the right of the *Landtag* or state parliament to propose bills, and the Ministerial Responsibility Act, which the Landtag could use to exert greater pressure on the ministers to carry out their duties properly. Three-year-old Ludwig, who had become the Crown Prince following his father's accession, had no way of knowing what consequences these changes were to have for his later reign. He was probably more concerned with the birth of his little brother on

27 April 1848. The boy was christened Otto. His mother Marie called him *»a first joy in these serious times«*.

These circumstances revealed the new Queen's strong piety, which was particularly evident in her letters and conversations. She considered God to be the head of the family and thanked Him earnestly for their good fortune. For her, the family was a refuge filled with joy. Records show that Maximilian also took pleasure in his children and spent a lot of time with his heir – something that was to change in later years. The Princes' parents both agreed that *»the earnest endeavours«* that they both considered of greatest importance needed to *»be built upon the foundation of religion«*.

However, this short-lived domestic bliss was repeatedly interrupted by the King's long absences (mostly in Italy). These travels abroad, ostensibly because of the monarch's health, met with little understanding among the court, ministers and people of Bavaria. In public, Marie only hinted at the unhappiness caused by these separations from her husband. However, her letters to Maximilian show that she suffered a great deal.

»THE CROWN PRINCE IS ALWAYS FIRST«

The two princes' early education was placed in the hands of Sybilla Meilhaus, who had entered royal service at the same time as Ludwig's wet nurse. The close relationship that developed, particularly with Ludwig, is shown by the very personal letters he wrote her, continuing even after he had become King, right up to her death in 1881.

Records show that the royal princes' education was extremely strict, almost puritanical. Meagre portions of food are mentioned, as are the severe punishments meted out after any boyish pranks. However, any evaluation of this needs to take contemporary views into account, when it immediately becomes clear that Maximilian's ideas on education were more or less the same as those held by the aristocracy in general. Children were to be brought up to be disciplined, modest and frugal. Thus there was nothing unusual about

Ludwig's education and the methods applied – apart from its particularly intense religiosity.

Sybilla Meilhaus obviously provided the children with the affection and understanding they lacked. Both she and many other servants were a key influence on Ludwig's later development and conduct: they reinforced the royal first-born's self-esteem to such a degree that Ludwig developed what seemed a natural sense of privilege over others: *»The Crown Prince is always first,«* as one of Ludwig's personal servants told him and those around him. Both his playmates and his brother Otto had to observe this rule. Gottfried von Böhm reported: *»On Sundays, aristocratic children of the same age as the Princes Ludwig and Otto were invited...The aim was to help both princes lose something of their inherent shyness. For this reason, playing at warfare and soldiers was particularly encouraged. Even in these childish games, the Crown Prince always wanted to be the first, and when they played the processions taking place on Corpus Christi, he already walked in the proud, stately manner typical of his later years.«*

Major-General Theodor Basselet de La Rosée should also be mentioned here; he was given responsibility for the princes' education in 1852, succeeding Sybilla Meilhaus. While one of his main concerns was to instil Ludwig, the future monarch, with a sense of the responsibility of kingship, he also emphasised the pre-eminent position that a royal ruler held in society. Ludwig's tutor possessed a marked sense of social class, leading him to impress upon Ludwig the importance of keeping his distance to his subordinates and behaving accordingly towards his servants. Even brother Otto was no exception; in spite of the brotherly affection between them, Ludwig made it clear that Otto was his *»vassal and subject«*.

But who was Ludwig at this point in time? Writing about the year 1851 in the family chronicle, his mother noted that *»Ludwig developed pleasure in art early on; he liked to build things, especially churches, monasteries and the like.«* Ludwig I continued to be a proud grandfather, reporting to his son,

Ludwig as Crown Prince. – Photograph (probably) by Joseph Albert, c. 1858.

King Otto of Greece: *»For Christmas 1852...Ludwig was given the »Siegestor« made of wooden building blocks for him to construct. He loves building, and I have seen him execute buildings excellently, surprisingly, and in good taste. I can see striking similarities between the future Ludwig II and the politically defunct Ludwig I...«*

These references to young Ludwig's interest in building are confirmed by many other contemporary reports. The young boy appears to have been strikingly imaginative and talented. Queen Marie wrote in her chronicle: *»Ludwig listened in delight when I told him stories from the Bible and showed him illustrations of them. The story of the woman of Samaria and the Sunday gospels appealed to him particularly strongly. He had a fondness for the »Frauenkirche« in Munich, liked to dress up as a nun, enjoyed play-acting, loved pictures and the like, liked being read books and told stories, and since childhood he has taken pleasure in giving his possessions, money and things to others.«*

We can already see the »Fairytale King« of later years starting to emerge from these reports and records. Ludwig's remarkable generosity in giving gifts in particular was to remain one of his traits until he died. That he never developed any real sense of money – another lifelong trait – was also evident in his childhood years. Ludwig was given only a small amount of pocket money, but thought that small sums would be enough to buy expensive presents, for example for his mother. He was greatly disappointed when his wishes could not be fulfilled through lack of money.

EARLY INFLUENCES

The royal family had several palaces where both they and their many servants could live. In winter they preferred to live in the the *Residenz* in Munich, while in summer they had a greater choice of stately homes. Hohenschwangau Castle in the Allgäu, which Maximilian had reconstructed from ruins when he was Crown Prince, was without doubt their favourite refuge. It is idyllically situated between two lakes in the foothills of the Alps, near Füssen. Ludwig II was probably influenced more strongly by this place than any other.

Besides Hohenschwangau, the royal family also had the use of Berg Castle on Lake Starnberg, Nymphenburg Palace (which at that time still lay outside the city) and Schleißheim Palace north of Munich – as well as other, more modest houses commissioned by Maximilian: he had had an Italianate summer house constructed on the *Roseninsel* (»island of roses«) in Lake Starnberg, close to the shores of Feldafing parish. This »Casino« was only completed in 1853, but was ready for use a year earlier. The Royal Villa in Berchtesgaden was built the same year as the »Casino«. Max, Marie and their two sons first stayed in the Villa in September 1854. It was ideally suited for longer periods of residence. As a child and young boy, Ludwig visited these places repeatedly, and it is here that he learned to love and appreciate nature.

»It is wonderful!« – Hohenschwangau Castle

»I am completely entranced by the mountains« is what Prussian Marie is supposed to have said upon seeing Hohenschwangau Castle and the surrounding Alpine landscape when her new husband Maximilian took her there for the first time at the end of October 1842. Maximilian's father Ludwig I was also completely delighted by the castle, writing to his son: *»Hohenschwangau is a veritable fairy-tale castle!«*

Maximilian had first seen the derelict former seat of the Lords of Schwangau as a 17-year-old while journeying through the area, and had bought it in 1832. By 1836, its reconstruction and internal repairs had progressed to the point where he could invite guests to stay; he himself stayed overnight in the castle for the first time in July that year. The main architect Domenico Quaglio (1787–1837), a painter of theatrical scenes and vedute, had designed Hohenschwangau in the Gothic style. The aim was to reconstruct this »historical monument«, and its Gothic form was regarded as a recreation of the castle's »original medieval appearance«.

Its location on the shore of the Alpsee and the backdrop of the Alps lends the castle, originally called »Schwanstein«, a very special atmosphere. Its comfortable interior design and many murals also contribute to its unique character. Hohenschwangau Castle is like a picture book of fairy tales and legends, of story and history, all connected or related to the castle's centuries-old site in the Schwanengau. From Charlemagne and the Nibelungs to Martin Luther, the rooms contain an educational wealth of images, both fact and fiction.

The *Schwanrittersaal* (»Swan Knight Hall«), which Ludwig, Otto and their parents used as a dining room, is decorated with scenes from the legend of the swan knight (that is, Lohengrin). As the castle and area's former rulers derived their name from the swan, it seemed acceptable to relocate the tale of the swan knight from its original setting on the Lower Rhine to the Alpsee.

The swan is regarded as the epitome of grace and dignity, and representations of the majestic white bird can be found throughout the castle – as paintings, embroideries or sculptures. A coat of arms bearing a swan hangs above the castle's main entrance, in the castle

gardens water flows from a swan fountain, and on the roof a large cast-iron swan holds a lightning rod firmly in its beak.
Young Ludwig would often sit up here gazing at the moon and the mountains, magically lit up by the light of moon and stars. It was only a few steps up from the rooms he and his brother had before they were moved to the newly built *Prinzenbau* (»Princes' Wing«) across from the main building in 1855. When their father Maximilian ascended the throne in 1848, the court grew and more space was required.
For Ludwig, the annual visits to Hohenschwangau were the highlight of the year. A letter written to his grandfather Ludwig I in 1861 gives a representative account of his experiences: *»We are having a very pleasant vacation here and are using the beautiful days partly for excursions, partly for fishing in the Alpsee, whose clear, mild waters are also extremely pleasant to swim in...Recently I caught an eight-pound pike, which I was so pleased about that I...had a photograph taken of it.«* In his many letters to his first governess, Sybilla Meilhaus (she later married and was called von Leonrod), he rhapsodised about how *»wonderful«* he thought Hohenschwangau was, stating that he had *»loved it since childhood«* as there he could discover *»a world of splendid memories«.*
Hohenschwangau Castle remained Ludwig II's favourite place of refuge until his death. It formed a base from which he could go riding and driving around the countryside. It was here that he first encountered the legend of the knight Lohengrin, who was sent by God, and here he drank in the world of fairy tales and legends.
One of the family's favourite excursions was to a cliff rising from the mountainside across from Hohenschwangau, where the ruins of the castles Vorderschwangau and Hinterhohenschwangau were located. It was exactly here, in place of the ruins, that Ludwig II

had his own castle built from 1868 onwards; this was the castle that was to become famous as Neuschwanstein Castle. The King kept an eye on the progress of the building works from Hohenschwangau using a telescope that can still be seen there today.

It was in 1854 that the young Princes Ludwig and Otto met the Danish poet Hans Christian Andersen for a second time. Andersen had been King Maximilian's guest on the *Roseninsel* two years previously. This time, the famous Dane stayed with the family at Hohenschwangau Castle, where he told the boys stories and made them paper cuts of comical soldiers and elegant lady dancers. Presumably he also recounted his popular fairy story »The Ugly Duckling«, which had become famous throughout Europe and told the tale of a misunderstood and ridiculed young swan. We can only guess to what extent Ludwig, who was misunderstood by his parents and those around him, saw himself reflected in the story.

Another influence, however, can be seen very clearly. The Crown Prince's favourite uncle was Adalbert (1828–1875), Ludwig I's youngest son. It was he who encouraged Ludwig's growing interest in literature, music, and theatre, and Adalbert was probably also the first to introduce his nephew to the poems and theoretical writings of Richard Wagner. Equally important for the Prince's development was the introduction his uncle gave him to French history of the 17th and 18th century. It was Adalbert who drew Ludwig's attention to the memoirs of the French politician and writer Louis de Rouvroy, Duc de Saint-Simon (1675–1755). These memoirs, widely read after their publication in 1829/30, provide the reader with a very personal, direct account of life at the court of the Bourbon King Louis XIV of France. Saint-Simon was one of Adalbert's and Ludwig's favourite reads.

For a certain time, Adalbert had hoped to become King of Greece as successor to his brother Otto, who had no children. In 1856 he married into the Spanish royal family and thus into the Bourbon dynasty. For this reason alone Adalbert devoted himself intensely to studying the divine right of kings as manifested in Bourbon rule. His nephew Ludwig shared his pleasure in courtly pomp and splendour and the ceremonies of the French royal court. And thus the foundations were laid for Ludwig's later affinity with France, which was to influence the architecture of his buildings (including Linderhof and Herrenchiemsee Palaces). Furthermore, after studying France's former absolutist monarchy, Ludwig became convinced that he had been chosen for royal office by God.

A comprehensive education is the foundation every monarch needs in order to rule well. Ludwig had accordingly been taught by private tutors from primary school age. Queen Marie reported of this time: *»Ludwig learnt and grasped things quickly, but he never enjoyed learning as much as Otto.«* Ludwig wrote to Sybilla Meilhaus from Hohenschwangau in the summer of 1854: *»Every day I have my lessons, just like in Munich.«* Two years later the subject-matter taught became considerably broader, as the subjects of the *Gymnasium* (secondary school) were added to the curriculum. Over the years that followed, Ludwig enjoyed his lessons in French, which he soon spoke very well (the Crown Prince wrote his first letters in French as early as 1856). From the summer of 1862 onwards, English words start to appear in Ludwig's letters (Ludwig to his cousin Wilhelm of Hesse: *»Otto does not know English.«*), which suggests he was taught English from this time. However, he never developed an extensive vocabulary in this language.

A LACK OF CLOSENESS

Even though Ludwig and Otto went on many walks in their mother's company, the warm, close relationship they had enjoyed with her for the first years of their lives evaporated. Maximilian's court secretary, Franz von Pfistermeister, noted that *»the Queen had only little understanding of how to draw the little Princes close. While she frequently visited them in their rooms, she did not know how to treat them in the way that children need to be treated. This did not endear her to her sons.«*

According to Pfistermeister's account, their father Maximilian had become similarly distant: »*The King...only saw Ludwig and Otto once or twice a day...He would usually only shake their hand in greeting and quickly take his leave.*« Taking Maximilian's absences, which often lasted for several months, into account as well, it is clear to see that the level of attachment between father and son, between the ruling king and his successor, was regrettably low. »*Even when the Prince was already nearly of age, it took considerable and lengthy effort to persuade the King to take his eldest son along on his morning walk through the Englischer Garten [in Munich] (from 9 to 10). However, this only happened a few times. The King said: what am I to say to the young man? He is not interested in any subject I suggest,*« Pfistermeister recorded. Ludwig later admitted in a confidential conversation with a Munich professor that he had not loved his father and had disliked the rigid Prussian education ordained by his mother, which had amounted to eight hours of torture that he had to bear each day. Even as a 33-year-old, he still complained to Crown Prince Rudolf of Austria that his father had always treated him condescendingly and had »*at most granted him a few cold words in passing*«.

»It is such a shame about Otto's ailing condition« – The king's brother

»*He is an utterly common person, without even the slightest sense of the high and beautiful. He often spends the entire day hunting, is much in the company of my shallow, vapid cousins and in the evening frequently attends the Aktientheater, where he is particularly enamoured of the ballet,*« Ludwig wrote of his younger brother Otto's lifestyle in a letter to Cosima von Bülow, Richard Wagner's mistress, in 1867.

The contrast between the two brothers was obvious from the beginning. It was not only in appearance that the tall, dark-haired Crown Prince and the much smaller and blond Prince Otto differed. In terms of their be-

haviour, too, serious, stern Ludwig and Otto, who initially was much more carefree and cheerful, might almost have been from two different worlds.
But though even in their children's games the elder brother made sure the younger knew which of them held the higher rank, there was no shortage of brotherly love between them. Many letters attest to Ludwig's great concern for Otto. Otto in turn was strongly attached to Ludwig, at least until he came of age, looking up to him in admiration. *»My first birthday away from Munich without my dear Ludwig, who sent a telegram,«* Otto wrote to his cousin Prince Wilhelm in a letter of 27 April 1865 from Berlin.
Otto's active service as a soldier in the 1866 Austro-Prussian war sent him into a depressed state of mind, and he became increasingly shy and unsociable. Otto's worrying mental condition was one of the reasons that Ludwig discarded his plans to abdicate at the end of 1870, as otherwise Otto would have become king. Ludwig wrote to Sybilla von Leonrod on 6 January 1871: *»It is such a shame about Otto's ailing condition, which is rapidly growing worse...he will often not go to bed for 48 hours at a time, he hasn't taken off his boots for 8 weeks, he plays terrible pranks, barks like a dog and has moments in which he hurls about the greatest incivilities; and then again he is often quite natural once more and as sensible as usual.«*
In January 1872, after Otto had been diagnosed with mental illness, Ludwig had his brother confined to Nymphenburg Palace. Otto complained to him: *»You have no right to tell me to go to this place or another within our territory, you have no right to treat me thus, for I have done no wrong...I have yielded only to force and am now a prisoner; I have been treated outrageously...I am now your prisoner until you see fit to grant me my freedom once again!«*
When Otto created a disruption during a church service in the Munich *Frauenkirche* in May 1875, accusing

himself of supposed sins, the freedom of movement and travel he had hitherto enjoyed was restricted considerably.
In 1879 he was interned in Schleißheim Palace and subsequently moved to Fürstenried Palace, where he died in 1916. Ludwig received regular reports on Otto's condition from the specialist psychiatrist Bernhard von Gudden; from 1875 onwards at the latest, the King feared he might meet the same fate as his brother.
After the death of King Ludwig II, Otto was nominally the King of Bavaria from 1886 to 5 November 1913. Because of his mental ill health, state affairs were managed by prince regents, first by his Uncle Luitpold from 1886 to 1912, and then, following Luitpold's death, by Luitpold's son Ludwig from 1912 to 1913 . Prince Regent Ludwig effected a change in the constitution that enabled him to rule as Ludwig III while Otto was still alive. Otto retained the title and ceremonial honours due to a King until his death.

Ludwig's passionate interest in literature and the works of Richard Wagner, which emerged around 1860, met with little understanding from his family and those around him. Likewise, no-one was able or willing to follow his vivid imagination, which often caused him to drift off into daydreams. The editor Ludwig Schaufert observed: »*It was at that time that the Crown Prince, who has such an ideal disposition, devoured our German classics in a state of joy that intoxicated all his senses and gave his bold imagination free rein, as they say. – It was then that he, sitting at his royal mother's feet, attempted to tell her of his enthusiasm and was bitterly disappointed when instead he was repeatedly brought back to cold, hard reality by that simple woman's prosaic and practical views.*«

Ludwig felt misunderstood, even rejected. This increased his penchant for literature, which for the rest of his life was to provide him with a means of escape from the here and now.

»TEARS OF RAPTUROUS DELIGHT«

On 2 February 1861, Ludwig was at last able to fulfil a long-held desire: he was able to see a performance of »Lohengrin« in the National Theatre in Munich. The fifteen-year-old Crown Prince was deeply moved as he followed the fateful story of the legendary swan knight, whose image he knew so well from the murals in Hohenschwangau Castle. On that winter's day, the son of Parzival, Keeper of the Holy Grail, became reality, taking on a body of flesh and blood through the singer's performance. *»The Crown Prince shed tears of rapturous delight over this, learnt the libretto and Wagner's other dramas off by heart in the solitude of his room and the park, and also avidly consumed Wagner's prose writings, especially his ›The Artwork of the Future‹,«* Gottfried von Böhm described the effect this visit to the opera had on Ludwig. Some years later, Ludwig confided to Richard Wagner that this performance of Lohengrin *»sowed the seed of Our love and friendship, which will last until death; from then onwards the spark of Our sacred ideals, which was soon to become a roaring flame, was lit in me.«*

It is no exaggeration to call this date, 2 February 1861, an important turning point, which determined the future King's entire thought, feelings, beliefs and creative endeavours from then onwards. As we shall see, Ludwig linked the mythical character of Lohengrin to ideas of divine right, kingship and purity through the Holy Grail.

As his coming of age drew nearer, Ludwig became increasingly involved in court society and the duties of a Crown Prince. His own account tells of his excitement on 4 February 1862, when for the first time he was to attend the *Kammerball*, a ball held specially for the young people at court. Around 180 guests waited eagerly to catch a glimpse of the tall, pale youth, or perhaps even to be presented to him. Uncle Adalbert was at Ludwig's side, which probably made it easier for him to converse confidently with other persons, many of whom were strangers to him. At any rate, Ludwig told his cousin Wilhelm from Darmstadt in relief: *»I danced everything.«*

»*To heavenly Darmstadt!*« – Close connections with Hesse

Unlike other German monarchs, King Ludwig II travelled very little. There were no official state visits or visits from his relatives during his lifetime. The family »of Hesse and by Rhine«, who ruled the Grand Duchy of Hesse-Darmstadt and to whom Ludwig was closely related, were the only ones with whom Ludwig developed a close relationship. Ludwig's deep attachment to his Hessian relatives began in childhood, and he cultivated their friendship until he died. He was in closest contact with his cousin Maria Anna (1843–1865) and his cousin Prince Wilhelm (1845–1900), the children of one of Queen Marie of Bavaria's sisters. Ludwig's friendship with Wilhelm lasted until the 1880s – the two visited one another and corresponded regularly.

Accordingly, Darmstadt was the only German capital that Ludwig got to know as Crown Prince and King. By contrast, the Bavarian ruler was never drawn to politically more important cities such as Berlin, Dresden, Stuttgart or Vienna.

The foundations of Ludwig's friendship with his Hessian family were laid in October 1861, when he spent over a week in Darmstadt with his mother. He visited the theatre almost every day, seeing operas, plays, a ballet and a *Singspiel* (musical comedy). The personal correspondence between Ludwig and Wilhelm, in which they wrote about their shared impressions of the theatre, shows that the two boys (who were nearly of an age) were brought together predominantly through their love of the performing arts and music. A few days after his return to Munich, Ludwig wrote to Wilhelm: *»You can imagine...how much we long for you and the happy days spent in Darmstadt, the most wonderful of our lives.«* The tone of the letters grows more and more dramatic, culminating in the wish *»If only I had wings, so that I could fly to you, to heavenly Darmstadt...!«* A year later, the Bavarian Crown Prince recalled *»for a second time the wonderful, wonderful days...we spent with you in beloved Darmstadt.«*

Shortly after Ludwig succeeded to the throne, Prince Wilhelm visited Munich for a period of several days, during which the two cousins visited the theatre together. Records show that Wilhelm visited Ludwig several times up until 1871. These visits were apparently always full of warmth and intimacy. *»Whenever I take the train to Starnberg, I recall that lovely day on which we sat together so cosily and drank coffee under the trees. I will never forget those days...«*, Ludwig enthused about one of his cousin's visits to Munich in 1867, during which the two of them took the opportunity to visit the picture gallery in Schleißheim Palace.

»I received such a dear, faithful, sympathetic letter from Ludwig...he has once again proven his true and rare brotherly love. He is the only real friend I have,« Prince Wilhelm wrote to his aunt, Queen Mother Marie of Bavaria, in 1885 after having received a letter of condolence from Ludwig. Although the two cousins seldom saw each another in later years, this strong attachment remained until Ludwig's death.

Beside Wilhelm, Grand Duke Ludwig III of Hesse (1806–1877) was also close to the Bavarian king, and was thus able to speak plainly to his nephew. When Ludwig stated that only a position similar to that held by the Czar of Russia was worthy of a king, the Hessian ruler replied, referring to political and constitutional reality: *»With that kind of opinion, my dear nephew, your Royal Highness should prepare to be cut down to size.«* The Grand Duke was to be proved right, as Ludwig II's later development would show.

Not quite three weeks later *»it was Kammerball again, where I enjoyed some pleasant conversations, and again last Tuesday, I always danced all the dances...two weeks ago today was the*

The brothers Crown Prince Ludwig and Prince Otto with Prince Wilhelm of Hesse (from right to left) in the atelier of court photographer Joseph Albert in the Karlstraße in Munich. – Photograph, 1864.

Artists' Ball in the Odeon, the third one we had seen. The hall was decorated beautifully...a splendid knight's castle arose in the background. The hall was very full.«

Nothing in these weeks suggested that Ludwig would withdraw from court and from public life and celebrations to the extent he did from 1871 onwards at the latest.

During the abovementioned Artists' Ball in the Odeon (a popular concert and dance hall built in the 1820s), Ludwig saw a decorative feature made by Christian Jank. Although he had no way of knowing it at the time, this theatrical painter was to become a most important artist for him: this image (»a splendid knight's castle«) from the 1862 Artists' Ball formed the basis for Jank's first design for Ludwig's castle project Falkenstein, 22 years later.

THE CROWN PRINCE – CHILDHOOD'S END

The only personal meeting between Ludwig and the Prussian Prime Minister Otto von Bismarck (later the first Chancellor of the Reich) occurred in August 1863. As Maximilian II was away, taking part in a meeting of German princes in Frankfurt, he gave his family the responsibility of receiving King Wilhelm I of Prussia. Bismarck himself described this meeting in his »Thoughts and Recollections« as follows: *»At the regular meals...the Crown Prince...was my neighbour at table. I had the impression that he...only occasionally remembered his intention of holding a conversation with me, and our talk did not go beyond the usual topics discussed at court. Nevertheless, I thought I could detect both talent and animation and a mind filled with his future in what he said...the impression he made on me was a congenial one...«*

Ludwig's mind may well have been somewhere completely different – perhaps on the celebration to be held a few days later, on 25 August, to mark his eighteenth birthday: in Hohenschwangau, the people came to pay homage to him upon his coming of age. Ludwig listed some of his birthday presents in a letter to his grandfather; they give us a clear picture of the Crown Prince's interests: *»A picture from the Church of All Saints, pictures based on the Nibelungs by Schnorr, a pin with a swan, a book on Faust and about the works of Shakespeare and others.«*

As further »presents«, Ludwig was now given his own apartment in the *Residenz* in Munich (where on moving in on 16 November 1863 he immediately hung up pictures of the swan knight Lohengrin) and his own servants, two orderly officers (one of them was Count Paul of Thurn and Taxis) and an aide-de-camp. Ludwig had already been allocated a modest appanage (stipend) a few weeks before his birthday. Moreover, he was now able to enjoy the unfamiliar freedom of being allowed to walk through Munich on his own for the first time. *»How quickly these 18 years have passed,«* Ludwig wrote to Sybilla Meilhaus, now married and called von Leonrod.

Theodor Basselet de La Rosée, who had been Ludwig's tutor for more than ten years, retired from this position when the Prince came of age. His verdict on Ludwig was: »*The Prince is bright and very talented, he has learnt a great deal and is already in possession of knowledge that goes far beyond the level desired. I have rarely encountered an imagination as rich as his in such a young man. But he is irritable and extremely vehement. His wilfulness, which is more than strong, suggests that he possesses an obstinacy...that will be difficult to curb.*« Ludwig indeed possessed this obstinacy, to which La Rosée had himself contributed.

On 20 September, like every previous Crown Prince coming of age, Ludwig swore an oath on the Bavarian Constitution. This also involved duties and expectations. The Crown Prince had to give a greater number of audiences and prepare for the lectures at the Ludwig-Maximilians-Universität starting in November. However, Ludwig's life as a student began with a setback. He became ill with a fever and sore throat and was forced to interrupt his studies in December.

On 10 March, King Maximilian II – who had been suffering from ill health for some time – suddenly died, and Ludwig succeeded to the throne as Ludwig II, completely unprepared for his duties. He had no learning apart from his general secondary education and the beginnings of his university studies (which he had not continued in 1864). He lacked completely the knowledge of national economy, constitutional law and theory of governance necessary to a monarch, nor did he know anything about military leadership or possess any experience of foreign countries and human nature. Nor did Ludwig have a fatherly confidant experienced in matters of state who could have taken the young King by the hand and led him.

»*...Poor Marie! But also poor Ludwig! Whose youth is now vanished, who has been put on the throne so soon at the age of 18, an age at which he can have no experience, no knowledge of business and all this in such times as these!...*« Ludwig I lamented to his son Prince Luitpold. And Marie? Shocked, she summed up the situation with the words »*Max died too young*« – both for herself and for her son.

»God will give me the strength
to carry out my difficult profession worthily!«

3 The first two years of Ludwig's reign

The 19th century was a time that hearkened back to the manners and events of the past. This was evident not only in new buildings constructed in the Classical, Romanesque, Gothic and Renaissance styles, such as the Town Hall in Vienna, the Capitol in Washington, D.C., or the Opera in Paris. In Bavaria, the public declaration of the new King's accession to the throne also took place in an archaic manner intended to imbue the ritual with meaning. On 10 March 1864, heralds in medieval garb rode through Munich on horseback to the sound of drums and trumpets. A crier, reading from a roll of parchment, read out the text proclaiming the new ruler from the House of Wittelsbach, the dynasty that had ruled Bavaria for centuries.

A day later, Ludwig II swore the oath on the Bavarian Constitution in the *Residenz*. His state of emotional upheaval had been too great for him to carry out this duty on 10 March, as originally planned. *»I swear to rule according to the Constitution and the laws of the Empire, so help me God and his Holy Gospel,«* Ludwig spoke before the assembled ministers, princes and higher state officials.

»What a lovable King, blessed with all of God's gifts! He has inherited a passionate love of the beautiful and the good from his forefathers, as well as a graciousness that delights and inspires his people. Possessed of ideal beauty, with a heart open to everything uplifting and moving, he takes the throne, worshipped by his people. He is the most popular of Kings!...«

Pope Leo XIII 1886 in his obituary for Ludwig

For those present at the ceremony, concern for Bavaria's future, given the young King's lack of experience, was

Heralds in medieval costume proclaim Ludwig as the new ruler of Bavaria in Munich on 10 March 1864. – Contemporary wood engraving.

balanced with affection for the tall, handsome monarch. The members of his family, above all, had very different ideas of what the future might bring. After all, from now on Ludwig was not only the Head of State, but also the Head of the House of Wittelsbach. He thus had the power to decide on all family issues (such as the marriages of the princes and princesses) and was the arbiter of financial and legal family matters.

The Berlin poet Paul Heyse, who had received much support from his patron Maximilian II, was among those worried about the future. Heyse admitted to his mother on 10 March 1864: »*...the country is quite literally orphaned, the young heir is mature only as far as his number of years is concerned, a good, harmless, delicate youth whose health is weak and who is an unknown quantity as far as his mind and character are concerned.*« In the same letter, Heyse (who was later to win the Nobel Prize for Literature) identified one of the key problems: »*His surroundings offer him no firm hold, no confidential adviser to look to; there is no statesman anywhere equal to this threatening and complicated situation.*«

However, on the day of Maximilian II's solemn burial, attended by several tens of thousands of people, these justified concerns were pushed aside in the face of his son's mourning. *»Ludwig's grief-stricken face naturally awakened everyone's sympathy and at once won the hearts of the people, who were suffering with him. If only you could have seen him, the pale young man, as he followed his beloved father's coffin with bowed head and faltering steps! His eyes are unusually expressive; in his uniform, his figure appears noble, I would even say regal...«* the singing teacher Julius Hey wrote about the funeral procession. The librarian Karl August von Heigel confirmed: *»The new ruler first won the crowd with his beauty...at least it was apparent to all present as Ludwig followed the coffin of his father, with bared head and slow footsteps. The women in particular were entranced by his large, dark eyes and their dreamy expression.«* A contemporary newspaper article also reveals how touched the onlookers and participants were by the youth: *»There can be no more affecting and heartbreaking expression of the deepest inner pain than that evident in the gait, countenance and conduct of King Ludwig II at the procession. The King's tall, slim figure looked bent, his gait was almost faltering and his noble visage was pale and covered in tears...but nevertheless his whole bearing remained manly, composed and distinguished.«*

For the populace, Ludwig's looks and bearing made him seem like a king out of a picture-book. Contemporary accounts and press reports called him a *»youth of ideal beauty«*, an *»imposing figure«*, and an *»Adonis on the throne«*. Above all, his expressive eyes seemed to capture the heart of nearly everyone who saw him.

»I have never felt as fresh as this« –
From radiant youth to royal wreck

»At last the door of the audience chamber opened to let me in...He stood only a few steps from the door in Bavarian military costume, carrying the feathered hat on his right arm. When looking at a person, one's eyes usually seek those of the other. And in his case, I could hardly tear my gaze away from his eyes, and everything else was taken in only at a glance, most of all his eloquent mouth,

around which there hovers the mark of his pure goodness of heart. His voice is low and sonorous, extremely soothing. His language is pure, unaffected German. My silent fear that I would find something sickly or overwrought in the crowned youth's character vanished at once; he is healthy and strong. His head moves delicately in a free and pleasing manner on his body, the proportions of which are taller than is usual; in short, every look, every word I recall today was only pleasant, only pleasing, had not the slightest touch of anything restrictive or oppressive. The dignity of a king paired with beauty and the expression of an undiluted nobility of soul, presenting a delightful sight that did me good to the very depths of my heart,« the composer Peter Cornelius, a companion of Wagner's, wrote in his diary in 1865 following an audience with Ludwig II. During the first two years of his reign, Ludwig was regarded as one of the most handsome monarchs on earth. His height (over six feet), his strong thighs, his beautiful, dark eyes and his wavy dark brown hair did not fail to affect men and women alike.

While the voluminous appearance of Ludwig's naturally straight hair was the product of daily hairdressing using curling tongs from 1863 onwards, his oft-mentioned eyes needed no extra embellishment. The Minister of Justice, Eduard von Bomhard, spoke of his *»truly magnificent eyes, full of intelligence and soulfulness«*, Paul Heyse was impressed by the *»beautiful large eyes, lit up with a dreamy glow«*, and Richard Wagner wrote of the *»magic of his eyes«*; a contemporary biographer wrote that Ludwig's manner of looking up through his lashes made a powerful impression upon women.

It is thus hardly surprising that the youthful monarch's portrait featured in many albums of verses and was worn by many women in their lockets. Reports also tell that some women would take cuttings of the hair of the horses that Ludwig rode, and that mothers would position their marriageable daughters in those parts of the Munich *Residenz* that were accessible to the public in the hope that the King would meet and fall in love with them.

This photograph is thought to be the last portrait taken of King Ludwig II. – Photograph by Joseph Albert, c. 1884.

Only a few years previously, Ludwig had been regarded as weedy, with a grey complexion and a head too small for his body. Ludwig was obviously aware of the latter, which is why he curled his hair to make his head look larger and in better proportion to his body size.

By all accounts, the King spoke in sonorous High German with a slight Bavarian colouring, and tended to pronounce his words in a somewhat rushed manner.

At first, Ludwig II was considered a very athletic man. As a child and young man, he often swam long distances in the Alpsee near Hohenschwangau and regularly rode out on horseback. In fact, during the first years of his reign Ludwig became notorious for his riding, remaining in the saddle for hours at a time: *»These long, wonderful rides enthralled me so much that I have never felt as fresh as this,«* he wrote to Sybilla von Leonrod in May 1864; later, he added: *»I can still feel the strengthening effect of these rides.«*

Ludwig was fully aware of how charismatic he appeared to others, which is why he constantly had photographs of himself taken. *»Incidentally, His Majesty has already been photographed 82 times, and there is still*

a huge demand. We should admire his tireless patience in these matters; what will he be able to achieve when the desire for more serious studies awakens in him,« Döllinger joked in a letter to Charlotte Leyden, the later Lady Blannerhassett, in November 1865.
Alas, the King's beauty vanished as quickly as it had come. Ludwig lost one tooth after another due to his poor oral hygiene. He grew fatter and fatter – in no small part due to his love of sweets – and in the 1870s was forced to give up riding following a hernia. In the 1880s he went on gentle walks, but for all other movement relied on being transported by railway, coach or sleigh.
When he died at 40, he was a physical wreck, far removed from the much-admired youth of former times. However, even though the loss of his looks must have pained him, there was one thing the aesthete Ludwig would not give up – being photographed.

FIRST STEPS AS KING

»You will not believe...how people are chasing after and clamouring for the young King's favour...«, wrote Maria Anna Gietl, the wife of the King's personal physician, to her son Max, one of Ludwig's former playmates, in mid-March 1864. The way in which the court officials and ministers sought to show themselves off to their new ruler did not escape the press outside Bavaria, such as the »Frankfurter Zeitung«: *»The ridiculous behaviour and disgusting flattery of those grovelling around the throne are likely to ruin the young king utterly and completely.«* According to the newspaper, these special attentions were being paid to a King whose features *»speak both of the unspoiled, sweet-tempered childlike nature and the naïve inexperience of the young monarch.«* However, Ludwig remained surprisingly composed in the face of such statements. He trusted entirely in God, as he wrote to Prince Wilhelm among others: *»My father's death was a heavy blow*

for us; God will give me the strength to carry out my difficult profession worthily!«

At first, the King kept on Karl von Schrenck-Notzing as his Minister of Foreign Affairs and the Royal Household as well as President of the Ministers' Council. However, one change was that Ludwig – unlike his father – had one of the six Ministers of State (Foreign Affairs/Royal Household, Home Affairs, Culture, Justice, Military and Finance) update him personally on how matters stood. Supposedly, »*how did my father do this?*« was one of the questions that Ludwig II asked most frequently. He wanted to avoid mistakes and show that he was up to the task of ruling; he wanted to be King, not only to bear the title. The Württemberg ambassador confirmed that »*All the people who have come into contact with His Majesty on matters of state business…agree that the King is fully aware of his difficult task and both feels and voices the urgent need to educate himself, does not shirk the effort needed to fulfil the duties of a regent, knows how to make the right judgements in many matters as much as is possible at present, is extremely conscientious and always anxious to be just in all decisions; however, in doing so (albeit not in cases of particular importance) he has proceeded in a manner that leads one to conclude that His Royal Majesty is not always guided by others, but wants to enforce His own opinion, even if it conflicts with that of the royal councillors.*«

The new King was credited with great eagerness. Breaking with his previous habits, he rose early in order to be able to receive the first secretaries at 8:30 a.m. He is supposed to have asked several times a day whether there were any ministers' proposals requiring his signature. Furthermore, according to the sources he had his meals served and cleared away quickly so as to be able to get back to work as soon as possible. Ludwig evidently carried out his tasks with a sure sense of current political issues, their requirements and the opportunities they offered. He was to retain this basic interest in political events until his death.

»The number of deputations is gradually shrinking; but I still have 1 or 2 hours of audiences every day, with which I am now quite familiar. – In the morning the secretaries come from 8:30 to 9:30 or 10. – Twice a week Hofmann [Court Secretary] comes from about 10 to 11; at 11 a different minister comes each day, then I take a second breakfast and usually around noon I grant audiences, go for a drive or walk; around 4 there is dinner, at 6 it is the turn of one of the secretaries, then Leinfelder [Cabinet Secretary Official] reads out the papers, which takes until around 9; then it is time for tea.«

Ludwig II to his former tutor nanny, now Baroness von Leonrod, 27 April 1864

In May 1864, Paul Heyse came face to face with Ludwig at an audience where the poet wished to thank him for continuing to pay the annual stipend granted by Maximilian II. On this occasion, Heyse thought he could detect that Ludwig had adopted a *»deliberately regal demeanour«*, which suggests that the young monarch had not yet settled into his role as King. But who could have offered him support and advised him on matters of state politics? In the same month that Heyse paid his respects, Ludwig received the composer Richard Wagner, whom he venerated, in a first audience. Here, at last, there was someone with whom he could talk about those topics that others did not understand. The »other world« that Wagner opened up to the King provided Ludwig with inner support, if only for the reason that the ministers were apparently trying to put him under pressure and force their will upon him.

Initially Ludwig sought a geographical escape to this situation by travelling to the spa town of Bad Kissingen in order to meet the King and Queen of Württemberg, the Emperor and Empress of Austria and the Czar and Czarina of Russia. This encounter proved so engaging that Ludwig extended his stay to nearly four weeks (and all involved repeated this meeting four years later).

Ludwig returned to Munich for only two weeks before departing once again to visit Czarina Maria Alexandrovna. He had become more closely acquainted with her in Kissingen, and now she was in Bad Schwalbach having additional spa treatments. After two weeks in Bad Schwalbach he travelled straight to Hohenschwangau, only returning to Munich for ten days at the beginning of October (where he went to see an opera or play nearly every evening). On 11 October Ludwig disappeared off to Hohenschwangau once more and only returned on 29 November; he stayed in Munich for the rest of the year.

At least the deeply unsoldierly King showed himself to his troops on 17 September 1864 on the *Marsfeld* (»Field of Mars«) before the Bavarian capital. After this first inspection of the army, for which Ludwig travelled to Munich specially, there were to be only very few meetings between the monarch and his soldiers. Furthermore – unlike his Prussian relatives – Ludwig throughout his life preferred to wear civilian clothes. The images of Ludwig in uniform that we encounter so often today do not correspond to historical reality. Indeed, Ludwig, the Supreme Commander of the Bavarian Army, must have made a comic impression when he visited Empress Elisabeth of Austria in Possenhofen, wearing his uniform and carrying an umbrella because of the rainy weather. He was not a military figure, and made no effort to hide this attitude.

As early as the autumn of 1864, it was increasingly being said that Ludwig II was exhibiting unusual behaviour. The Austrian ambassador Gustav Blome reported back to Vienna: *»The young King is still a problem, there are still the strangest contrasts in his behaviour, it is impossible to predict what he will be like when the fermentation of his character, which at present is manifesting itself in such different ways, is complete…«* – referring mainly to Ludwig's tendency towards introversion. However, the young King was still carrying out all expected tasks, showing himself to the audience at the Munich Court Theatre and publically attending church for the first time at the Boxing Day service at the Court Church of All Saints. The public watched him carefully and noted every detail.

At the same time, towards the end of 1864 demands increased for the King at last to summon the *Landtag* – that state institution through which the King could symbolically and visibly enter into a relationship with the people through their elected representatives. However, Ludwig did not want any gathering of these delegates to take place. His own personal condition was of greater interest to him than the important message conveyed by the summoning of parliament that he was ruling *»in the spirit of the Constitution«*.

»You would like my rooms« – Ludwig's early buildings

A few months after his succession to the throne, the young King had alterations made to the bedroom in Hohenschwangau Castle previously used by his father. *»You may recall,«* Ludwig wrote to Sybilla von Leonrod in August 1864, *»that there are orange trees painted on the blue ceiling. So as to enhance the illusion that I am outdoors, I have had a fountain with real water installed in the room, which looks really well; it was possible to do this without leaving any traces of damp in the room. – An artificial moon is also being made, as are orange trees. So the impression and the illusion will have a pleasant effect upon those who see it.«*

Thanks to these installations and a rainbow machine, the so-called Tasso Room became transformed into a cabinet of technical wonders. At the same time, natural outdoor phenomena that the King could have experienced right outside the castle walls were brought indoors. For example, flickering light shone through small holes in the ceiling, which were filled with crystal glass; this light came from an oil lamp placed in the room above. This light was supposed to imitate the stars glittering in the night sky.

With his new bedroom in Hohenschwangau, Ludwig for the first time made real one of his own building and decorating ideas, and – as would also be the case in the years to come – used specialists from the theatre to do so. For Ludwig II, theatre and construction were two directly related areas that went hand in hand with one another.

This project – his »journeyman's piece«, as it were – in Hohenschwangau was followed the same year by the construction of a representative hallway to Ludwig's chambers in the Munich *Residenz*. He continued to use the apartment he had lived in as Crown Prince after his succession due its comparatively secluded location (Ludwig I had actually had special royal living quarters built in the so-called *Königsbau* (»King's Building«) on the south side of the *Residenz*). The walls of this hallway, which was around 30 metres long and ran parallel to the Residenzstraße, were adorned at the King's behest with thirty scenes from Richard Wagner's music drama »The Ring of the Nibelung«, which were painted by Michael Echter between November 1864 and 1866.

In 1867, this *Nibelungengang* (»Nibelung Hallway«) was followed by three further commissions for building projects within the Munich *Residenz*. The rooms that Duchess Sophie in Bavaria was to occupy following her marriage to Ludwig were decorated in the French style of Louis XV. Ludwig insisted that Fontainebleau Palace (60 kilometres south of Paris) be used as a model for the design of the furniture and the fabrics chosen. At the same time, the King had his own chambers completely redecorated, as he described to Sybilla von Leonrod towards the end of December 1867: *»I think you would like my rooms, if you saw them again, I am having them done up in the rich, magnificent style that was fashionable when Louis XIV was on the throne; they make a sumptuous and splendid* *impression, but without losing their characteristic cosy, liveable feeling. They will be completely finished only in the summer.«*

In the same letter, Ludwig also mentioned the third construction project, a conservatory taking up about 30 square metres on the roof of the so-called *Hofgartenbau* (»Court Garden Building«): *»Next to the small, sky-blue study I have had built a small conservatory, which has turned out absolutely delightfully.«*

However, neither this little conservatory nor the King's chambers, which had only just been finished, were to remain the same for long. Towards the end of 1868 Ludwig was already giving orders for his chambers to be altered once more. Following their completion in the summer of 1869, they were even more magnificently decorated than before, with a well-nigh unsurpassable number of ornaments and sculptured decorations. From now on, an image of the sun and its rays, the symbol of the French Sun King Louis XIV, adorned the head of the bed; busts of this ruler and of Marie Antoinette decorated the bedroom; and the fresco on the study ceiling showed »Apollo with the horses of the sun, and Night fleeing from the light.« Ludwig wrote of this to Sybilla von Leonrod on August 1868: *»One will feel completely transported back to the period of Louis XIV, to the time of the splendour of Versailles, which at that time was the most magnificent, splendid royal seat in Europe.«*

Ludwig II had the first, small conservatory replaced with a semicircular, free-standing and self-supporting glass and iron structure that took up the entire roof space of the *Hofgartenbau* – over 1300 metres. Completed in March 1871, the result was a conservatory of impressive size, which at the same time was also one of Ludwig's most fantastical buildings. However, neither this nor any of Ludwig's other early building projects have survived.

The King's audience chamber in his private apartment in the north-west corner pavilion of the Munich Residenz. – Photograph, late 1930s.

The only item that can still be seen today is the device of the artificial moon described by Ludwig in his letter, which is still hanging from the ceiling of the royal bedroom in Hohenschwangau.

CONFIDENTIAL CONVERSATIONS

At the end of the first year of his reign, the King was giving his Cabinet Secretary Franz Seraph von Pfistermeister cause for concern. His duties disgusted him and he preferred studying and philosophising to enduring the *»plain and prosaic«* people around him. For this reason, the Cabinet Secretary asked the Munich professor Johannes Huber to visit the Munich *Residenz* regularly to talk to the King about philosophy, religion, politics, social matters and personal problems. These meetings took place in Ludwig's chambers.

In his twenty or so meetings with the King between December 1864 and May 1865, Huber discovered that the monarch felt *»the demands imposed by his artistic ideals were misunderstood by those around him«* and that he thus preferred to lead *»the kind of life of a hermit.«* The professor experienced a King who thought little of *»the masses«*, but at the same time was captivating in his *»winning charm«*, as he noted.

According to Huber's recollections, Ludwig II had a tyrannical streak: *»There is without doubt something sinister about him,...but I will tell the King at the next opportunity that one can only educate oneself to become a liberal prince and avoid the risk of becoming a tyrant if one has respect for other men. Sadly, his surroundings are not suited to teaching him respect for mankind.«*

It is not known whether Huber put his plan into practice. Be this as it may, he was able to get to know Ludwig II well enough to sketch his character in a way that captured some of the King's essential contradictory traits quite early on. The monarch was both lively and cordial and cool and distant, combining charm and ruthlessness, searching for reality and longing to escape from the world. Furthermore, Huber wrote, Ludwig had a realistic grasp of events, a well-developed imagination and excessive notions of his own power. At the same time, there were situations that made the King feel insecure on a personal level.

In the autumn of 1864, Ludwig effected a change of leading Minister, and thus was able at least to send a signal of his power and of his resistance to the ministers' conduct, which he saw as improper. Karl von Schrenck-Notzing was replaced as Minister of Foreign Affairs and the Royal Household (and thus as leader of the Ministers' Council) by Ludwig von der Pfordten. Von der Pfordten had already been leading Minister of Bavaria between 1849 and 1859.

At this point, the young King was thus still fairly politically active. He looked at all instructions given to foreign ambassadors, was interested in internal political processes and was provided with in-depth reports on ongoing issues by his ministers and secretaries.

DREAMY AND UNPREDICTABLE?

In 1865 Ludwig held a reception and concert at court to mark the New Year. Three weeks later, the King confessed in a letter to Sybilla von Leonrod that he was already limiting the previously high number of audiences he gave: »*As always, I see a minister every day and am now giving audiences twice a week; thus I have gained time to read, which always gives me great pleasure...on the whole I live in seclusion as much as possible...*« He complained to Ludwig von der Pfordten: »*Every day shows me anew that this corps is well on its way to becoming a power hostile to the Crown. To me it thus seems imperative that it be put in its proper place and that the limits of its power are clearly drawn. I do not fail to recognise the difficulty of this task; I expect much of your support.*« Here, the monarch expressed his dissatisfaction with the entire bureaucracy and at the same time indicated how powerless he felt himself to be. Less than a year after his accession to the throne, Ludwig II had only one answer to this: instead of putting on a show of power and taking more decisive action to effect change, his latent desire to withdraw from it all became stronger. It almost amounted to a flight from official business and his representative duties.

At least the King now finally summoned the *Landtag*, which he opened in person on 27 March 1865. Prior to this, however, Ludwig and the President of the Ministers' Council, von der Pfordten, had clashed over the date – with the result that Ludwig was seriously put out and refused to speak with his leading Minister in person for weeks. In addition, he was confined to his bed due to illness for a lengthy period of time, which increased his desire for greater freedom beyond the confines of the city. »*At this point,* [the King] *could still present me with his doctors' recommendation that he seek seclusion. For this reason I will remain silent this summer, but then I will have to do my duty and present myself to him,*« von der Pfordten wrote, still exercising patience with Ludwig II. The King however was already thinking about »*devoting myself to serious study in the coming winter.*«

Thanks to the ambassador of the Kingdom of Hanover, Ludwig von Ompteda, we have a report of how matters stood on 30 June 1865: »*The King is currently residing in Berg. I have heard consistent reports from various sides that His Majesty is isolating himself even from those closest to him and takes pleasure mostly in long, intense rides, even expeditions on horseback lasting several days, travelling strictly incognito and accompanied only by a groom.*«

Likewise in the summer of 1865, the theology professor Ignaz von Döllinger, who was very close to Ludwig, reported to Charlotte Leyden: »*Our young man is becoming increasingly dreamy and unpredictable.*« Four months later, he wrote to the same confidante: »*He would like most to spend this winter, too, in quiet and seclusion, without any public appearances; however, he has been told emphatically that this will not do for various reasons, that he must not attract the displeasure of the ladies and the masses engaged in trade, that is, that he will have to take part in balls, court concerts and so on. I hope he will comply.*«

This wish was not to be granted. Despite his marked sense of majesty, Ludwig failed to make use even of the options available to him as a constitutional monarch. Disillusioned and disappointed by reality, he had long since decided to create his own world: artists and craftsmen were already busy redecorating rooms in the Munich *Residenz* and in Schloss Hohenschwangau at great expense – even though the first signs heralding the fateful year 1866 were already visible, when Ludwig was to face his first great test as King of Bavaria.

»True artist by the grace of God«

4 Ludwig rescues Richard Wagner

Richard Wagner arrived in Stuttgart at the end of April 1864, on the run from his many creditors. He wrote to his friends: *»I need a good, a truly helpful miracle,«* and *»I am at my wits' end,«* revealing the measure of his desperation.

Only a few weeks previously, Wagner had stopped off in Munich: *»It was Good Friday; the weather was harsh, and the entire population...seemed caught up in the atmosphere of this day. Only a few days ago King Maximilian II, whom the Bavarians loved so dearly, had died, leaving his son as heir to the throne at the youthful...age of 18 ½. In a shop window I saw a portrait of the young King...which moved me with the particular emotion awakened in us by beauty and youth in what we suspect to be extremely difficult circumstances,«* the composer wrote many years later in his autobiography.

On this March day in 1864, Wagner could as yet have no inkling that this young King had been reading – in fact, downright devouring – his theoretical writings and opera libretti. Ludwig's enthusiasm for Wagner's operas and the myths woven into them was so great that he was constantly searching for further reading that explained the composer's oeuvre and dealt with the myths in greater detail. The scion of the House of Wittelsbach was particularly interested in »Lohengrin«, »Tannhäuser«, »Tristan and Isolde«, and »The Ring of the Nibelung«, of which only the text was available at this point.

In his preface to the »Ring«, which consists of four operas (»Rhinegold«, »The Valkyrie«, »Siegfried« and »The Twilight of the Gods«), Wagner had developed the idea of a *Festspielhaus* or festival theatre. Linked to this was the expectation that a prince or nobleman would provide the necessary financial support. Wagner qualified this with the sceptical query: *»Will this prince be found?«*

As early as the autumn of 1863, Ludwig had entertained the idea of searching for Wagner and inviting him to his court, but he only put this plan into practice once he had become King. He asked his Cabinet Secretary, Franz Seraph von Pfistermeister, to discover Wagner's whereabouts, and simultaneously scoured the list of arrivals in the city of Munich. Nobody knew who or what the King was searching for.

After searching various cities in vain, Pfistermeister finally tracked Wagner down in Stuttgart and handed him a personal letter, a ring and a portrait of the King. Wagner was both surprised and overjoyed, and eagerly accepted the invitation to travel to Munich the following day and meet Ludwig. *»My dear, gracious King! I send you these tears of heavenly emotion to tell you that now the wonders of poetry have entered into my poor, loveless life as divine reality! – And this life, its every last verse and note, now belongs to you, my merciful young King: you may dispose of it as your own possession! In greatest joy, faithfully and truly your servant,«* Wagner wrote in a letter sent to Ludwig from Stuttgart.

On 4 May 1864, Wagner – short of stature, 51 years of age, speaking in Saxon dialect – stood before tall King Ludwig II, who was more than 30 years his junior, in the Munich *Residenz*. Each was probably as excited as the other. The author, poet and musician whom Ludwig admired so greatly and referred to constantly in his letters and diary entries was now standing before him in the flesh at last. And Wagner was anxious to see whether this meeting would lead to the realisation of all his as yet unfulfilled wishes and plans.

»LOYAL TO HIM FOREVER«

Both Ludwig and Wagner described their first meeting in letters to third parties. On the same day, Ludwig wrote to Duchess Sophie in Bavaria, one of Empress Elisabeth's sisters: *»If only you could have witnessed how much his gratitude shamed me when I gave him my hand, assuring him that his great work about the Nibelung would not only be completed, but would also be performed as he himself wished, that I would ensure faithfully* *that it would come to pass. At this, he bent low over my hand and seemed touched by this, even though it was only natural, for he remained in this position for some time without saying a word. I felt as if our roles had been reversed. I bent down towards him and drew him to my heart, feeling as if I were speaking a solemn oath to myself: I will be loyal to him forever...*« And Wagner wrote to a friend: »*Alas, he is so beautiful and gifted, soulful and magnificent, that I fear his life must fade away like a fleeting, divine dream in this cruel world. He loves me with all the ardour and passion of first love: he knows everything I have written, and understands me as if he were my own soul. He wants me to stay with him forever, to work, rest, and perform my works; I am to complete the Nibelungs, and he will perform them exactly as I wish. I am to be my own master, with no restrictions, not a conductor, nothing other than myself and his friend...*«

In the nineteen years that followed (until Wagner's death in 1883), the poet-composer and the monarch exchanged around 600 letters and telegrams, most of which were taken up with descriptions of their respective feelings and states of mind (taking precedence even over the exchange of ideas and information). Even the forms of address used by the King in his letters to Wagner – »*Beloved, only friend!*«, »*My dearest love!*«, »*You my only one! Holy one!*«, »*My one and all! Embodiment of my delight!*«, »*Noble, divine friend!*« – clearly reveal the intensity of his emotions. It would be wrong, however, to infer any kind of romantic attachment from this overblown language; there was nothing of the kind. Ludwig's devotion to artists and art was marked by exaggerated pathos in his language, which was influenced by and included a large number of poetic quotes (for example by Caldéron, Dante, Goethe, Grillparzer, Hugo, Schiller, Shakespeare and Wagner). And Wagner reacted to Ludwig's exuberance with equal pathos, partly out of calculation, no doubt – even though he was sometimes overwhelmed by the King's overly poetic choice of words.

During the first weeks, Ludwig and Wagner saw each other almost daily, first in Munich and then in Berg Castle, where Ludwig and his royal household moved for two weeks in mid-May 1864. Ludwig offered his friend Villa Pellet near Kempfenhausen on Lake Starnberg, which he had rented specially, as a place to stay. Berg was easily accessible from there.

»It is so close to the city that everything can be done as easily as if one were there« – Berg Castle on Lake Starnberg

Visitors to one of Ludwig's favourite places of residence encountered a surprisingly modest, unadorned building: this was Berg Castle on Lake Starnberg, which at that time was still often called *Würmsee* (»Lake Würm«). Robert von Mohl, the ambassador of the Grand Duke of Baden, described his impression of the King's life in this country seat after having been summoned there for a final audience in 1871: *»The castle was small, cramped and exceptionally plain, even the room of the King himself...I knew full well that the King was living in Berg Castle all on his own...But I was still surprised to find the castle completely unguarded and without any kind of order or supervision...While I was waiting, I looked at...the rooms on the castle's first floor. I thought them very plain, containing only minor artefacts or none at all. In the corridors and courtyards various house servants, kitchen boys, and chambermaids were milling around, all dressed in most unsuitable clothing... In short, the combination of kingly bearing, monastic seclusion and the disorderly lifestyle of a bachelor was extremely odd.«*

For Ludwig, who had known Berg Castle since childhood, this residence offered two important advantages: it was situated in the midst of nature, not far from the mountains, but also within easy reach of Munich. *»I am planning...to go to Berg, and enjoy the pleasant quiet and country air... - It is so close to the city that everything can be done as easily as if one were there,«* the

King wrote to Sybilla von Leonrod in 1864.

The main façade of Berg Castle on Lake Starnberg with the tower »Isolde« built by Ludwig. – Coloured photograph, c. 1887.

The building's design is simple. It has three storeys and a pyramid roof, and has belonged to the Wittelsbach family since the 17th century. While its park, designed as an English landscape garden, dates back to Max I Joseph, the small private harbour is one of the features surviving from the time of Maximilian II. The building's most striking architectural features – the neo-Gothic additions to the exterior and two towers, all commissioned by Maximilian II – were added in the 19th century, giving Berg the look of a proper castle. All of these features were removed after the Second World War. The only change made by Ludwig II was the addition of a third tower on the castle's north front, which he named »Isolde«. Ludwig did, however, leave his mark on the castle's interior design. He had the rooms decorated with a large number of paintings of scenes from the works of Friedrich Schiller and Richard Wagner (Ludwig also had small alabaster statues of Wagner's heroes set up). Furthermore, he had a number of smaller buildings constructed in the park, including the conservatory formerly in the Munich *Residenz*, a grotto, a Gothic chapel and a kiosk in Oriental style. The most interesting thing of all was the steamboat that Ludwig had inherited from Maximilian and renamed »Tristan«.

Ludwig often used it for boat trips on Lake Starnberg, frequently to the *Roseninsel*. On the return trip to Berg, »Tristan« (the boat) would draw close to »Isolde« (the tower), a reminder of Wagner's opera »Tristan and Isolde«, and its tragic story of unfulfilled love. In 1886, after Ludwig II had been deposed, he was held prisoner in Berg Castle and actually died not far away. Following his death, the castle was at first opened to the public as a museum, completely unchanged. It has been the private summer residence of the Wittelsbach family since 1949.

This place, where Ludwig once enjoyed the greatest freedom, reminds us today both of the moments in which that freedom was turned into captivity and of his tragic end.

On 18 May 1864, Wagner wrote to an acquaintance about the days he spent in Berg: *»I am now reading my poetry to him; he eagerly seeks to be instructed about everything that has remained unclear to him, with soulful enthusiasm and wonderful perceptiveness; his concern and involvement are often very moving: his beautiful face shows the deepest pain and greatest delight, depending on what mood I put him in…«* For both the King and Wagner, these were days of joy (*»Wonnetage«*), with piano playing and philosophising among their pastimes. Until September 1864, when Wagner moved into the villa in Munich's Brienner Straße provided for him by the King, the country house by the lake remained his refuge; he was followed there by the composer and conductor Hans von Bülow and his wife Cosima (née Liszt) and the conductor Karl Klindworth. They, too, became acquainted with the King and played to him on the piano. Hans von Bülow, whose wife had been having an affair with Wagner since November the previous year, was given an honorary stipend as the »King's piano player«.

In financial terms, it was Wagner who profited the most from the King's generosity. In addition to other gifts and donations, from May 1864 onwards he was paid an annual salary of 4000 guilders (the same salary as a ministerial councillor), while in June 1864 he was given 16,000 guilders as a gift and later that year his removal costs of 4000 guilders were paid. In the summer of 1865, there followed an annual sum of 1200 guilders to keep a coach and horses; from November 1867 he was paid an annual salary of 8000 guilders, and in March 1869 given a loan of 10,000 guilders, for which the King waived repayment each year. Ludwig also granted Wagner money for holidays, gave him many expensive gifts and permitted him to use the royal locomotive for trips to Italy. This catalogue includes only a small part of the total payments and expenses, all of which were paid for by Ludwig II out of his own pocket. Ludwig thus proved his determination to keep his promise to save Wagner from destitution and *»drive the lowly concerns of everyday life...away from you forever«* at all costs.

OUTLINES OF A CULTURAL POLICY

The poet-composer was to finish his incomplete works and prepare the supposedly unperformable opera »Tristan und Isolde« for the Munich stage (the premiere in Vienna had been cancelled after 77 rehearsals). At the beginning of October, Ludwig and Wagner discussed one of the King's childhood dreams: Wagner was to compose the »Ring of the Nibelung«: *»we will give this wonderful work to the German nation and show both Germans and other nations what German art is capable of!«* Wagner signed a contract stating that he would complete the operas within the next three years. In return, Ludwig paid him the requested fee of 30,000 guilders. Some of this money was used to top up Wagner's annual salary. In exchange, Ludwig was given all rights to the whole of the »Ring«.

One of Ludwig's other main concerns at this time was the implementation of a cultural policy, for which he had drawn up some rough outlines. Without having sought the advice of state institutions or ministers, he had come to the conclusion that the people needed to be educated and enlightened through high art. In a letter to his composer friend written on 8 November 1864, Ludwig expressed it thus: *»It is my aim, through the performance of more serious and important works, such as those of Shakespeare, Calderon, Goethe, Schiller, Beethoven, Mozart, Gluck, and Weber, to put the Munich audience into a more elevated, composed frame of mind, to gradually wean them away from those common, frivolous, tendentious plays and thus to prepare them for the miracle of your works, and facilitate their understanding of them by first performing the works of other distinguished men; for all must be filled with the gravity of art.«*

»PALACE OF THE FUTURE«

A few weeks later, Ludwig announced he wanted to *»have a large, stone theatre built in Munich, for the perfect performance of the ›Ring of the Nibelung‹. This incomparable work must be provided with a space worthy of presenting it...in short, the sentence that you use in your preface to the poem ›The Ring of the Nibelung‹, is to come to life...«*

Gottfried Semper was engaged as the architect of Ludwig's first great building project. Along with his friend Richard Wagner, Semper had taken part in the 1849 May uprising against the Saxon king in Dresden. While Wagner's ideas for the theatre saw it as something more provisional, Ludwig envisioned the heights above the river Isar with *»a street crowned by the palace of the future«* – very large and made of stone. This building project ultimately failed because of political and social resistance in Munich. The population had never before seen a single musician being given such support, and regarded Ludwig's patronage of Wagner with resentment and jealousy. Wagner, too, became less and less convinced that the kind of theatre the King desired corresponded to his own ideas for a festival theatre. In the end it was Ludwig II himself who decided that he would not and could not take any risk with the substantial funds needed, given the climate of opposition. *»O, the blind masses, who fail to grasp the significance of this work,«* he lamented, and in

Ludwig II discusses the model of the planned Wagner festival theatre in Munich with the architect Gottfried Semper (standing) and the composer Richard Wagner (sitting). – Drawing by Hans Stubenrauch, c. 1920.

January 1866 still confessed: »*I frequently visit the heights of the Isar; it breaks my heart when I think that the building I long for will never be erected there…*« Ludwig's first building project had thus failed. He was never again to plan any public building for Munich on his own initiative.

Many years later, however, the basic architectural concepts of Semper's building were a significant influence on the *Festspielhaus* built by Wagner (and partly financed by Ludwig) in Bayreuth.

Preparations for »Tristan and Isolde« went on unimpeded, however. Wagner directed and conducted a successful performance of »The Flying Dutchman« in December 1864, and not quite six months later there followed the triumphal first performance of the »unperformable« opera. That which had failed in Vienna succeeded in Munich on 10 June 1865. The enthusiastic audience had already given the opera rousing ovations in the dress rehearsal. Ludwig himself was so overwhelmed by the performance that he reprieved all non-Bavarian revolutionaries of an 1849 uprising in the Rhine

Palatinate. This was also an indirect reprieve for Richard Wagner, one of the builders of barricades in Dresden in 1849.

»Without him the performance never would have happened. He urged it, focusing all of his energy upon it, and Wagner's triumph is truly his,« one reviewer wrote of King Ludwig; many similar comments can be found in contemporary newspaper reports.

> *»And when the two of us are no longer, our work will still serve as a shining example to posterity, an example that will delight for centuries to come, and hearts will be kindled in admiration of Art, Art that comes from God, Art that lives forever!«*
>
> *Ludwig II to Richard Wagner on 4 August 1865*

FIRST CRACKS

However, dark clouds were gathering over the friendship between monarch and artist. At the beginning of the year, Wagner was the subject of heated debate in the public sphere. The media accused the composer of exorbitant demands, extravagance and attempting to influence the inexperienced young King politically. While Wagner no doubt considered that he was simply being suitably recompensed for his work, his next request for a sum of 40,000 guilders added fuel to the flames. Wagner wrote to the King: *»You should give in a royal manner, and leave the matter of how I should someday return this royal trust to my conscience!«* His demands were granted. Ludwig's officials took their revenge by paying out large parts of this sum in cash. Cosima von Bülow, coming to collect it, was forced to hire a second carriage to transport the sacks of money.

Wagner, popularly known as »Lolus« in a play on the name Lola Montez, mistress of Ludwig I, met with great resistance among the ministers. Cabinet Secretary von Pfistermeister in particular, who had been the one to track down Wagner, now distanced himself from the composer and explained to Ludwig that he risked alienating his people with his intense devotion to Wagner. Wagner himself railed against von Pfistermeister and the King's advisors, and attempted to influence the King directly in his decisions concerning the staff on a ministerial level.

The final straw came when Wagner returned to Munich after a week's visit to Hohenschwangau and anonymously claimed in the newspaper »Münchner Neueste Nachrichten« that *»the removal of two or three persons...would at one swoop liberate the King and the Bavarian people from...irksome vexation.«* Ludwig von der Pfordten spoke clearly to his King: *»Your Majesty now stands at a fateful crossroads and has to decide between the love and worship of your faithful people and the friendship of Richard Wagner...«* Ludwig was forced to react: the entire ministry threatened to resign if Wagner was not exiled. The King's relatives, led by his mother Marie, also put pressure on Ludwig because of the precarious position in which he had placed the royal family. As Ludwig II visited the theatre one evening, the audience hissed at him.

EXILE IN SWITZERLAND

At the crack of dawn on 10 December 1865, Richard Wagner followed the orders he had received from the King four days previously and left Munich, accompanied only by his manservant and his dog. He took the train to Switzerland, where he continued to draw the agreed annual salary by Ludwig. *»We will never give up the friendship that binds Us! – I was forced to act as I did for your own peace,«* Ludwig justified himself to the composer.

Richard Wagner, who saw Ludwig as an important ally in turning the renovation of culture he desired into reality, ultimately settled in Tribschen near Lucerne. The King travelled there on 22 May 1866 to congratulate Wagner on his fifty-third birthday, despite Bavaria's being in the middle of a politically challenging situation of crucial importance to its future. The public reaction to the visit was catastrophic. But Ludwig could not and would not give Wagner up.

In June 1867 there came about the first serious disagreement between the two, over who should be cast in the title role in the new Munich production of »Lohengrin«. Ludwig would not accept the 60-year-old singer whom Wagner had chosen for the role, as this man failed completely to embody his ideal image of the swan knight. Ludwig attended the dress rehearsal together with Wagner, who in the meantime had briefly returned to Munich, but left the theatre without speaking a word to him. Wagner was offended and left for Tribschen. On 16 June 1867, a much younger tenor sang the part of Lohengrin – exactly as Ludwig had wanted.

Even though Ludwig wrote a letter to Wagner a few weeks later, in which he thanked him for the good wishes he had sent for the King's birthday, and addressed him as *»O my beloved friend, for me my real birthday is the 4th of May, and the 22nd...«*, thus underlining how important the day of their first meeting and Wagner's own birthday were to him, the tone of his letters became more reticent.

The year 1868 initially brought another triumph for this odd couple. On 21 June the curtain of the Munich National Theatre was raised for the premiere of the »Mastersingers of Nuremberg«. The audience was thrilled and the opera was a huge artistic success. Wagner sat beside Ludwig in the royal box and bowed to the cheering audience – a great honour for the middle-class former revolutionary. Wagner found his own way to thank the King, who had spent more than 45,000 guilders from his own private coffers on performing the »Mastersingers«: he gave Ludwig the original score of the opera for his birthday. However, this was to be the last high point in the relationship between the poet and his patron. They were not to meet again for another eight years – eight years that left their mark on their relationship.

»That is where the oak of my true love for you is rooted« – In search of Lohengrin

»I had a letter sent to Berchtesgaden, where I...saw a young man working in a sawmill, who struck us all with his beauty and heroic form, I will have him...photographed in Berchtesgaden and then...have him painted as Lohengrin,« Ludwig told Sybilla von Leonrod in an 1863 letter. Ever since boyhood, Ludwig had kept a constant eye out for men whose outward appearance matched his vision of the swan knight and could serve as a model for depictions of Lohengrin. Ludwig was convinced that the Grail Knight, son of the Grail King Percival, a messenger of God and symbol of chivalry, could only be a young, handsome man. This explains his clash with Richard Wagner in June 1867 over the casting of an older singer in the part of Lohengrin.

In Ludwig's eyes, the mythic figure of Lohengrin was first and foremost the son and heir of Percival, the keeper of the Holy Grail. In the myth, the Holy Grail is linked to Christ's death and resurrection. However, there are many different ideas of what the Grail, which according to medieval legend is kept in a castle named Montsalvat, really is. Ludwig always had it depicted as a bowl or cup (usually along with the Holy Ghost in the form of a dove). The Grail appears in the Percival myth (Wagner gave the name »Parsifal« to the hero of his last opera) and in the legends of Lohengrin as one of these two objects.

»During our drawing lesson, Otto drew soldiers celebrating, and I the scene in which Lohengrin reveals his identity,« Ludwig informed Wilhelm of Hesse in January 1863, showing how different the two brothers' interests were. A few months later, on Good Friday 1863, Ludwig copied out parts of the story of the Grail from Richard Wagner's opera »Lohengrin«. In the following years, it became a ritual for the King to repeat this every Good Friday. For Ludwig, Good Friday equalled the certainty that his sins, too, had been forgiven through the death and resurrection of Jesus.

In the spring of 1864, shortly before his father's death, Ludwig wrote a poem titled »Vision«, in which the Crown Prince gathered a kind of brotherhood of

Grail knights around himself and became their king – the parallel to Lohengrin and Percival is clear. However, in marked contrast to this imaginary vision of the King of the Knights of the Holy Grail, the bitter reality of life as a constitutional monarch was to hit Ludwig a few weeks later when he ascended the throne of Bavaria.

The public was well aware of the Bavarian king's love of the figure of Lohengrin and the eponymous opera. Rumours abounded, for example, that Ludwig would on occasion dress up as Lohengrin himself. Thus it is hardly surprising that Ludwig II is often referred to as »Lohengrin the Second« or »King Lohengrin« in private and diplomatic correspondence of the time.

We do know that in November 1865 Ludwig had »the scene of the swan knight's arrival from Wagner's opera Lohengrin [re-enacted] upon the Alpsee«. The chronicle of Hohenschwangau Castle describes it thus: »A large swan, artfully modelled upon nature, drew a barge with Lohengrin (aide-de-camp Prince Paul of Thurn and Taxis)...; the swan knight...was splendidly lit using electric lights. During this procedure, the musicians played the respective pieces from Lohengrin. This scene was repeated the following evening, on the highest order of His Majesty the King.«

In »Lohengrin« »the oak of my true love for you is rooted,« Ludwig declared to Richard Wagner at the beginning of their relationship. This is why he wanted to have »Lohengrin« performed in Munich in May 1866 to mark the composer's fifty-third birthday. Unfortunately, the only singer whom the King thought suitable for the title role, Albert Niemann, was unavailable and the performance did not take place. In 1876 in Bayreuth, Ludwig was still very enthusiastic about Niemann, whom he called »the first among the singers and actors«.

On 13 June 1886, the day of Ludwig's death, the curtain of the Vienna Court Opera (now the State Opera) lifted at 7 pm for a performance of »Lohengrin« with Albert Niemann in the title role. According to official reports, at more or less the same time as Ludwig's body was discovered in Lake Starnberg, the tenor, whom the King had called a »supernatural figure«, was singing: »My beloved swan! Alas, how gladly I would have spared you this last, sad journey! – ... Farewell! The Grail will be wroth if I remain here!«

In 1866, Wagner urged Ludwig to issue a formal statement in the Bavarian newspapers to dispel rumours of a relationship between the composer and Cosima von Bülow. Ludwig did him this favour, trustingly assuming that there was no adulterous affair going on between Cosima and Wagner. Towards the end of 1868, however, the fact began to dawn upon him that Wagner had taken advantage of him and his royal position. Cosima admitted her love for Wagner to him in writing. By the day of the first orchestral rehearsal of »Tristan and Isolde« in April 1865, she had already given birth to their first child, passing her off as Hans von Bülow's daughter. Wagner's second daughter was born in February 1867. Ludwig saw how greatly he had been deceived, but nevertheless wrote to Cosima in March 1869: *»You cannot know how true and passionate my affection for you is, for apart from our friend you are the creature I hold most dear, most venerable on this earth.«*

ALIENATION

Despite this pathos, the King was now much more distant in his dealings with the couple and stood upon his royal privileges more than ever before. Thus, against Wagner's wishes, he demanded that the premieres of the operas »Rhinegold« on 22 September 1869 and »Valkyrie« on 26 June 1870 take place in Munich. The composer saw himself robbed of his vision of staging perfectly the four separate operas of the entire »Ring of the Nibelung«, in a location where the technical and artistic equipment was adequate for his requirements. He was also quite horrified by the production. Ludwig in his turn stressed his position as the one holding the rights to the works.

Wagner forbade Hans Richter, who was employed at the Court Theatre and paid by the King, to conduct »Rhinegold«. Ludwig lost his temper completely, telling his court secretary that the *»conduct of Wagner and this theatrical riff-raff is truly delinquent and shameless; this constitutes an obvious revolt against My instructions, which I cannot tolerate...the people of the theatre must obey my orders, not Wagner's whims.«*

In 1870 – Ludwig was now even threatening that »[Wagner's] *works will never again be performed on the Munich stage«* – the monarch saw no merit in having the composer present at the rehearsals and premiere of the »Valkyrie«. Thus Wagner attended only the final performance, where his dislike of the Munich production was amply confirmed.

Six years later, with the opening of the *Festspielhaus* in Bayreuth and the first complete performance of the »Ring of the Nibelung« (which was also the premiere of the operas »Siegfried« and »Twilight of the Gods«), the composer's long-held dream came true. During August 1876, many distinguished people (among them Anton Bruckner, Edvard Grieg, Friedrich Nietzsche, Camille Saint-Saëns, Leo Tolstoy, Peter Tchaikovsky, the German Emperor Wilhelm I and Emperor Pedro II of Brazil) flocked to the small Franconian town in which Wagner had now taken up residence. At the laying of the first stone of the theatre on 22 May 1872, it had still been unclear whether this mighty project would succeed. King Ludwig sent a congratulatory telegram, which was immediately bricked into the foundations. However, Wagner's hopes that the King would provide a royal guarantee for the building of the Bayreuth theatre were dashed. Nevertheless, when the whole »stage festival« threatened to founder due to lack of funds, Ludwig stood surety for a large sum of money. *»Our plan must not fail!«* he declared.

Despite this, the King was not among the guests at the premiere in 1876. He preferred to attend the dress rehearsals when the house was empty, sitting at Wagner's side in the royal box. As soon as the curtains fell upon the »Twilight of the Gods«, Ludwig departed. He sent Wagner a euphoric letter from Hohenschwangau: *»You are a human god, the true artist by the grace of God, who brought the divine spark from heaven to earth to cleanse it, beatify it, redeem it!...My rejoicing soul will praise you, heavenly one, now and always!«*

Ludwig was so enraptured that he returned to Bayreuth from 27 to 30 August 1876 to attend the third performance of the »Ring« cycle – once again at Wagner's side, overcoming his dislike of the great publicity engendered by this event.

The next encounter between Ludwig and Wagner, which was to be their last, took place in 1880. On 10 November they attended a performance of »Lohengrin«, followed by a harmonious meal *à deux*. Their time together ended in discord, however. On 12 November Wagner complied with the King's request to conduct the prelude to the as yet unfinished opera »Parsifal« a second time. But when Ludwig demanded that this be followed by the prelude to »Lohengrin« so he could compare the two, Wagner handed the baton on to another conductor and left the National Theatre, greatly affronted. The next day he refused the King's invitation to go to a performance of Verdi's »Aïda« and instead attended a different event. Thus, somehow fittingly, it was indeed at a performance of »Lohengrin« that the King and the composer saw each other for the last time. Ludwig and Wagner continued to correspond after this as if nothing had happened. They indulged in reminiscences of their times together and discussed the soon to be completed *»Bühnenweihfestspiel Parsifal«* (»sacred festival drama Parsifal«). Ludwig did not attend its premiere at the second Bayreuth festival on 26 July 1882. His dislike of human company had increased still further, and he preferred to see the opera in a performance given in Munich – for himself alone. This, too, antagonised Wagner, who thought that »Parsifal«, which represented the pinnacle of his artistic achievement, should only be performed on the stage of the Bayreuth *Festspielhaus*. On 20 January 1883, the King informed the composer that, given the contractual agreements between them and the funds he had made available so that »Parsifal« could be completed, this royal request was wholly justified and that he insisted it be complied with. On 13 February 1883, not even a month later, Wagner died in Venice. Ludwig was shaken and stated, confidently, that the *»artist who is now mourned by the entire world was first recognised by me; I saved him for the world.«*

The dramatic works of Richard Wagner, which Ludwig had known and taken to his heart from his youth, rendered myths and legends accessible to him. At the same time, they provided him with ideals with which to counter harsh reality. The elevation of life through art was Ludwig's dearest wish, and he placed great importance on the Christian virtues that Wagner had made the subject of his works. Ludwig was convinced that certain musical and poetic works (including those of Friedrich Schiller and William Shakespeare) had a cathartic effect on their audience – and thus on himself. Richard Wagner's works corresponded exactly to the King's world of ideas and his artistic sensibility. And this affinity was to influence and become manifest in all of Ludwig II's creative endeavours and, indeed, in his entire life.

It is certain that without the patronage and understanding of Ludwig II of Bavaria, Wagner would never have been able to complete many of his operas, let alone have them performed. Ludwig's generous support had less to do with Wagner as a person, however. The decisive factor was rather that Ludwig was the first to realise that Wagner was an artist of exceptional ability and to recognise the value of his work.

»I will not be a powerless shadow king!«

5 1866, the year of change

The forced separation from Richard Wagner in December 1865 cast the King into a state of despair. He saw himself abandoned by his confidant and misunderstood by those around him. *»I am suffering terribly...I feel completely alone, alone on the royal throne, surrounded by the glow of princely splendour, a fire that gives off no heat...«*, he wrote to Cosima von Bülow on 2 January 1866. He enquired repeatedly after Wagner's well-being, made plans for their joint future, and continued to cling to his ideas for the construction of the Semper theatre in Munich. At the same time, the King's tendency towards introversion and withdrawal increased, usually taking the form of trips to Lake Starnberg and Hohenschwangau or to the mountains. This tendency also manifested in illness, which prevented him from carrying out his representative duties and audiences, and – whether intentionally or not – frequently occurred when Ludwig II felt cornered or threatened. This was the case in the spring of 1866, when he repeatedly complained of *»slight nausea«*.

»Our royal master is living wholly in the realms of legend, poetry, music and drama. His world is the theatre, which for him is the epitome of all splendour. He wants nothing to do with the rest of the world, with the prose of life, and would like to keep himself as far away from it as possible,« wrote the theology professor Ignaz von Döllinger in February 1866. Ludwig's lack of leadership qualities did not escape public notice. Even though the tension between Prussia and Austria was nearing breaking point, the Bavarian monarch still hoped that everything would somehow turn out alright. In reality, however, matters were more serious than ever: the struggle between Prussia and Austria for political supremacy in Germany required that Bavaria, too, take decisive action.

LOOMING WAR

Ever since the German Confederation had won the 1864 war against Denmark over the Duchies of Schleswig and Holstein, the future of these territories had been contested. Although the issue of sovereignty had been regulated by treaty, Prussia, which was responsible for Schleswig, occupied Holstein, which was under Austrian administration. The aim of Prussia – led by Otto von Bismarck – was to exclude Austria from the German Confederation and thus establish Prussia as the leading German power. Bavaria opposed Prussia's violation of Confederation law through its occupation of Holstein. In the end, despite having entertained other plans in the meantime, Bavaria stood by its alliance with Austria. The idea of a closer association of the German powers as a counterbalance to the two major powers of Prussia and Austria, which had been proposed by Maximilian II in 1864 and which would have included Schleswig-Holstein as an independent state, stood little chance in 1866.

In February, Minister von der Pfordten impressed the seriousness of the threat of war upon the King. However, the peace-loving monarch, who in any case was in the midst of a personal crisis because of Wagner, rejected all thoughts of combat, stating repeatedly that he did not want there to be any armed conflict. Ludwig hated fighting in all its forms, and he had never accepted war as a way of taking political action and expanding power.

On 15 May 1866 he reacted with utmost horror to the entire ministry's appeal that the *Landtag* be summoned and the Bavarian army mobilised. He spoke openly of abdicating in favour of his brother Otto, who was now of age, and of moving to Switzerland – to Richard Wagner. However, when Ludwig voiced this desire to Wagner by telegram, the composer was greatly concerned. Presumably Wagner feared that Ludwig would no longer be able to provide him with the same level of financial support if he put his plans into action.

Probably for this reason, Wagner suggested to his patron that he should completely give up *»any concern with art, with*

Portrait of Ludwig *II.* – Photograph by Joseph Albert, 1865.

our plans« for half a year, and instead dedicate himself *»to state affairs…with greatest energy«*, open the *Landtag* and show himself to the people.

On the evening of 22 May, a certain »Walther von Stolzing« presented himself at the door of Wagner's new home in Tribschen. Ludwig II, accompanied only by a squire, had secretly set out from Berg Castle under a false name in order to wish his master a happy birthday.

»I cannot help doffing my hat to Schiller!« –
The poet's influence on Ludwig II

Ludwig's spontaneous trip to visit Richard Wagner in Tribschen near Lucerne in May 1866 was not his first journey to Switzerland. During the autumn of 1865, he had spent around ten days on Lake Lucerne in order to visit the *»Rütli«* (an alpine meadow where according to legend the Swiss Confederation was founded in 1291), a chapel built in honour of the Swiss freedom fighter William Tell, and the *»Hohle Gasse«* (a ravine between Immendorf and Küssnacht where Tell is supposed to have shot the Habsburg reeve Hermann Gessler).

The play »William Tell« by Friedrich Schiller (1759–1805), which the King had performed on 18 October 1865 in the National Theatre in Munich, inspired Ludwig to visit in person the settings of the individual events it portrayed. Ludwig had revered the poet Schiller and his works from the age of eleven.

Although Ludwig's reaction to Schiller's works continued to be a strongly emotional one, as the years went by he increasingly emphasised the poet's importance for his cultural policy. *»The theatre must be brought back to its original purpose. – It must be a place of education, not a place to entertain the frivolous, hedonistic masses«*: this was the King's programme as expressed to Sybilla von Leonrod in 1865 – much as he had put it to Wagner the previous year. The works of Friedrich von Schiller were to assist the implementation of these cautious first attempts to formulate a cultural policy. Schiller's works were performed frequently and unabridged at the National Theatre at the King's command. These plays, including »William Tell«, »Mary Stuart«, and »Don Carlos«, lasted up to six hours and were followed by Ludwig with an intensity that the majority of those in the audience were unable to share.

To the King's mind, Schiller's works would educate the people, ennobling their characters and rendering them more receptive to *»great and lofty«* matters. Ludwig's ideas about religion and the workings of God played a decisive role here, too. He preferred art that he believed to contain the commandments of God, or to lead to God. Ludwig thought that Schiller's plays, like Wagner's music dramas, dealt with ideals of Christian virtue that it was his duty to encourage among his people through performances of the plays.
Ludwig knew most of the texts off by heart, and felt that the works of the *»immortal Schiller«* (Ludwig II in 1880 to Anton von Hirschberg) provided him with help and consolation. In »Don Carlos«, for example, the heir to the throne is urged to use all his powers for the good of his people: *»Tell him, in manhood, he must still revere / The dreams of early youth.«* These lines formed the subject of a letter that Ludwig wrote to Cosima von Bülow in March 1867: *»These words* [of Schiller's] *have always moved me deeply. I vowed I would follow them faithfully. With pride, with a pure conscience I can say that I have kept my vow faithfully, and neither can nor will I ever break it.«*
In his letters, Ludwig often quoted from literature, not least from Schiller's works. Another example dates from 1876, when he wrote to the actress Marie Dahn-Hausmann: *»By and large I am happy and content, that is, when I am in the country, in the splendid mountains – I am only ever miserable and downcast in the unholy city. I cannot live in the rank dungeon air; liberty to me is breath! Even as the alpine rose grows pale and withers in the swampy air, there is no life for me but in the sun, in the balm of heaven's refreshing breeze. To stay long here, in the city* [Munich], *would be my death!«* The last lines are nearly identical to a passage from the fourth act of »William Tell«: *»Even as the Alpine rose / Grows pale and withers in the swampy air, / There is no*

life for him, but in the sun, / And in the balm of heaven's refreshing breeze. / Imprisoned? Liberty to him is breath; / He cannot live in the rank dungeon air!« Another oft-quoted statement by Ludwig is also nothing other than a slightly extended quotation: *»I want to remain an eternal mystery to myself…«*, says Beatrice in »The Bride of Messina« – and Ludwig added in the same letter to Dahn-Hausmann, *»and to others…«*
Around the year 1880, there was even a phase in the construction of Neuschwanstein Castle, which the King had started building in 1869, during which the plans for the King's chambers included murals depicting scenes from Schiller's works. In the end, however, Ludwig decided against William Tell, Don Carlos and Mary Stuart in favour of pictures from the works of Richard Wagner. Nevertheless, the King's interest in Schiller's works continued unabated. His last journey away from Bavaria took him back to Lake Lucerne. He travelled there in the summer of 1881 with the actor Josef Kainz in preparation for a new production of »William Tell«. They stayed for over two weeks, and the young actor was forced to recite passages from various works by Schiller, from »William Tell« most of all.

A DISAPPOINTED PEOPLE

Ludwig returned to Berg on 24 May. When he opened the *Landtag* in person in Munich three days later, the Bavarian people gave him the cold shoulder. *»On the ride to church on the day of the opening of the Landtag, the public did not cheer him, indeed, he was scarcely greeted at all,«* Chlodwig zu Hohenlohe-Schillingsfürst recorded in his memoirs.

The greeting accorded the King by his members of parliament was also *»icy cold«*, as Ludwig noted. They knew that the King had deferred the date originally fixed by the ministry for summoning the chamber by two days – because he as sovereign had not authorised it in advance and presumably also because it conflicted with his travel plans. Ludwig had declared in a letter of 21 May that he had no *»plans to* [travel] *any distance worth mentioning«* – only to depart for Switzerland the very same day.

It is easier to understand the tension in the kingdom when we take into account not only the King's support of Wagner, but also the great disappointment of the Bavarian people that Ludwig had still not travelled around his own country. He had been King of Bavaria for over two years, and still thought there was little need for him to get to know his country or show himself to his people and his soldiers. Bavaria was composed of several very different regions, as well as the Palatinate, which lay beyond its main borders, and it should have been imperative for Ludwig to present himself as a leader capable of integrating all of Bavaria's disparate parts.

Ludwig II was not very popular with many of his subjects. The euphoria which had greeted him at the beginning of his reign had long since vanished, and the King himself was responsible for this. This made it all the more important for him to speak before the parliament, as anything else would have been interpreted as a rejection of his citizens and a lack of interest in his kingdom's fate. But Ludwig apparently placed no importance on any real cooperation with the two houses of parliament. This is evident from the fact that he opened the *Landtag* in person, with a King's speech, only three times over the entire course of his reign.

»DEEPLY UNFORTUNATE TIMES!«

Prussia withdrew from the German Confederation, and on 16 June 1866 Prussian troops invaded Hanover, Electoral Hesse and Saxony, breaking up the confederation of sovereign states that had been formed in 1815 following the fall of the Holy Roman Empire of the German Nation (to give it its full official title) in 1806. The Bavarian ministerial council was in favour of supporting Austria, as Austria was defending the Confederation and its law. So now there were thirteen states loyal to the Confederation – including Bavaria – against eighteen secessionist states.

When the Austro-Prussian War began, Ludwig was staying on the *Roseninsel* with Paul von Thurn und Taxis, his personal assistant in military and ceremonial matters, and a squire. The monarch had quite literally fled there. On 11 June the three men celebrated the anniversary of the premiere of »Tristan and Isolde«. Although the King refused to see any ministers, ambassadors of the Imperial Council or his Cabinet Secretary, important documents were brought to him by boat, at least. The King was well informed, in fact, and in possession of detailed information on the entire conflict over Schleswig and Holstein. But Ludwig was unable to commute his knowledge into practical governance. He continued to make himself unpopular through his well-nigh childish behaviour. Although rumours of what was going on upon the island abounded, his ministers were gradually becoming accustomed to his conduct. In any case, they were able to reach decisions and thus govern with hardly any interference from the King.

»O, deeply unfortunate times!« Ludwig telegraphed to Richard Wagner from the *Roseninsel* before returning to Munich. At the end of June, he managed to visit his main army headquarters in Bamberg. The young monarch's charisma worked its magic during the two-day visit: Ludwig was greeted with enthusiasm. But this demonstration of kingship remained an isolated episode: while elsewhere battles raged fiercely, Ludwig once more withdrew to Berg Castle and the *Roseninsel*, seeking *»the necessary peace and composure«*.

DEFEAT AND PLANS OF ABDICATION

News of the Austrians' crushing defeat at Königgrätz reached the King in Berg on 3 July and the report of the defeat of the Bavarian troops near Kissingen a week later. The victorious Prussians crossed the River Main and reached Nuremberg, raising their black and white flag over the Imperial Castle.

»God grant that Bavaria's independence can be preserved; if not,...if we end up under Prussia's hegemony, then away, I will

not be a powerless shadow king!«, Ludwig wrote in desperation to Richard Wagner on 18 July. More statements with thoughts of abdication followed, some of them to those closest to him. Döllinger wrote to his confidante Charlotte Leyden that the King would *»rather...chop wood or abdicate than deal with the business of ruling and cooperate with the ministers.«* But the topic of abdication was also mentioned from a different perspective: *»I look to the future of Bavaria with a heart full of fear...Our young King...is not in the least concerned with the highly critical circumstances of our time... You will see, it will end with an enforced abdication,«* were the prophetic words of Prince Karl, Ludwig's great-uncle and Commander in Chief of the Southern German troops, in a letter to his brother Ludwig I. The Viennese newspaper »Neue Freie Presse« circulated the following story: *»When Prince Karl returned home and the King could not be moved to greet either him or his troops, a family council was held in which the question was raised of whether King Ludwig has sufficient talent to rule Bavaria, or whether it was necessary to make it possible for him to leave the throne and withdraw into his private life, where he could live out his affection for Wagner undisturbed and without any risk to the country.«*

If this family council did indeed meet, they certainly did not suggest to Ludwig that he abdicate. Rather, Wagner and his mistress Cosima von Bülow through their letters helped to dissuade Ludwig from his own plans, which went in the same direction as those purported by the newspaper. The composer's words *»Kingship – believe me! – is a religion! A king believes in Himself, or He is no king!«* struck a chord in Ludwig II and resonated with his understanding of himself as a monarch. *»Wonderfully strengthened, feel a hero's courage in me, will bear it,«* Ludwig replied in a telegram.

PRUSSIA'S TRIUMPH

An armistice was agreed on 28 July. In the peace negotiations that followed, Napoleon III of France interceded successfully on behalf of the Southern German states. He was interested in maintaining a buffer zone between his own country and Austria and Prussia. Thanks to the efforts of the French, and contrary to the Prussians' original intentions, the Bavarians got off lightly in these negotiations: a payment of 30 million guilders in compensation for war expenditure and the cession of only a few territories. The secret military pact agreed with Prussia weighed much more heavily. This pact set out mutual military support between the two states and specified that in the event of war the Bavarian troops would be placed under Prussian command. The ministers agreed, even though Ludwig insisted on the complete integrity of Bavaria's territory and state sovereignty. This alliance of »*Schutz und Trutz*« (»protection and defence«) between Bavaria and Prussia, which the King was unable to prevent, marked a fundamental change in Bavaria's position. Austria's withdrawal from the German Confederation and the dissolution of the Confederation meant that the political order of Germany was realigned, with Prussia as the leading German power.

Ludwig II was not naïve. He saw the threat to his country and his crown quite clearly, and he knew what duties he should have faced up to. Furthermore, he feared that a coup could be staged against him. But he was too weak and insecure to draw the proper conclusions and bring himself to take convincing action.

Thus it was at first very difficult for Ludwig's ministers and advisers to persuade him to travel to those parts of Franconia that had suffered the most from the War. Was it Wagner's threat that he would reject the King forever if he could not bring himself to act that brought about Ludwig's change of heart?

On 10 November 1866, Ludwig II departed on a one-month journey through his kingdom. It became a triumphal procession, and the King deployed all of his charm, enhanced by his radiant good looks. He himself reacted euphorically to the rapture he elicited among the people – his subjects. During his visits to Aschaffenburg, Bad Kissingen, Bamberg,

Fürth, Hof, Nuremberg and Würzburg, Ludwig appeared chivalrous, gallant and a complete gentleman. We should not forget, however, that it was mainly the higher officials of the respective towns and cities who came into direct contact with him.

CHANGE IN MUNICH

While Ludwig's retinue of more than 100 persons, ninety-three horses and seventeen state coaches travelled across the country by railway, the political quarrels in Munich were escalating. Ludwig von der Pfordten, after the King had refused to grant him an audience several times, handed in his resignation on 13 December. He followed Cabinet Secretary Franz Seraph von Pfistermeister, who had been fired by Ludwig in October. *»Pfi and Pfo are now powerless,«* Ludwig reported happily to Cosima von Bülow, stating that Wagner was now free to return to Munich thanks to the sacking of his greatest opponents. Towards the end of the year, Ludwig appointed Chlodwig zu Hohenlohe-Schillingsfürst as the new President of the Ministerial Council. Zu Hohenlohe-Schillingsfürst was Prussian-friendly and self-confident, and under his presidency the antagonism between the pro-clerical and patriotic ministers and the more liberal forces increased.

Although Ludwig himself had anti-clerical tendencies, he wanted the Church to help him redress the loss of sovereignty he had incurred through the War: he asked the Vatican to include a daily prayer for him in their celebration of Mass. The Church rejected this request, however, stating that it was inappropriate and the King could also be prayed for after Mass. The idea – so important to Ludwig – that the granting of this request would somehow enable God to support him more strongly, was in keeping with his espousal of a Christian ethos of kingship. *»God will show me the path I must take…I will defy the demonic powers, I will obey the inner, the infallible holy voice, I will be guided by it alone,«* he declared to Cosima von Bülow.

»Thanks be to God, this terrible event did not come to pass!«

6 Betrothal to Sophie in Bavaria

In the weeks and months that followed the Battle of Königgrätz on 3 July 1866, the King was frequently to be found among the guests at Possenhofen Castle, the summer residence of the Dukes in Bavaria, where he discussed the current political situation with his *»faithful, beloved friend«* Duke Karl Theodor in Bavaria (1839–1909). Karl Theodor's sister Sophie was also staying at Possenhofen. She was eight years younger than the Duke and the only close relative of Ludwig's who was interested in Wagner. The siblings, another of which was Elisabeth or »Sisi« of Austria, were the children of one of Ludwig II's great-aunts and thus his second cousins (or »second-degree aunts and uncles«, as the relationship is called in German). The King felt comfortable and at ease in this familiar and sympathetic environment.

The general atmosphere at Possenhofen and the great sympathy that Sophie, who was very musical, had for Wagnerian opera were probably the reasons that Ludwig frequently sent letters and bouquets of flowers to his younger »aunt«. During Ludwig's suffering following his separation from Richard Wagner, she became his confidante, someone to whom he could speak openly about the composer. She understood him and he was happy to have someone he could talk to.

Sophie's mother Ludovika, however, had no comprehension of the infatuation with Wagner which Ludwig and Sophie shared. She suspected that the frequent meetings between the Bavarian King and her unmarried daughter were motivated by reasons of a completely different nature. During tea at Possenhofen on 12 August 1866, Ludovika demanded unequivocally that Ludwig make his true intentions known. After all, as Sophie's mother it was her duty to prevent potential bridegrooms from getting any false ideas about the Empress of Austria's sister. Clearly agitated, Ludwig left their company. Ludovika then sent her son Karl Theodor to visit the King in Berg Castle to try and find out more, using his position as Ludwig's close friend.

When Ludwig declared that he was certainly not thinking of marriage, Sophie's mother forbade any further correspondence between them – but neither Ludwig nor Sophie obeyed. They were able to exchange their thoughts freely only through letters, as propriety and the conventions of the time meant that they were always chaperoned when they met in person in Possenhofen.

In January 1867, it became noticeable that Sophie appeared to have fallen in love with her second cousin. She asked Ludwig to observe her mother's ban on correspondence so that she could gain some detachment – otherwise she would have to consider entering a convent.

»COMPANION OF MY THRONE«

On 19 January, Ludwig bade farewell to his confidante with the moving words: *»Oh, bear no grudge against me in your heart, dear Sophie, hear my plea and remember me fondly in your heart, do not take your friendship away from me...live happily and think of me.«* Three days later, they were betrothed.

During the brief period between their parting and reunion as an affianced couple, Ludwig had met his cousin at two balls. The sight of Sophie, whose health was clearly suffering, evidently touched him so greatly that in the early hours after the second ball he asked his mother to speak to Sophie on his behalf. *»Will you be my wife? Companion of my throne? Queen of Bavaria?«*, he asked Sophie in a letter. On 22 January 1867, she replied with a clear *»Yes!«* The public were made aware of this unexpected development the very same evening, when the King asked Sophie to join him in his royal box at the theatre.

»How overjoyed I would be to hold your firstborn, my great-grandchild, in my arms,« Ludwig I wrote to his grandson, joining in the chorus of congratulations and celebration among

the Bavarian people, the ministers and the couple's families. While many of them would have preferred the King to marry into a higher-ranking family than a side branch of the Wittelsbachs (in 1864, there had been unfounded speculation that Ludwig was going to marry a daughter of the Russian Czar), the beautiful Sophie was nevertheless accepted – especially as a son and heir was needed.

At the same time, those familiar with the King and the court were sceptical. The decision appeared very sudden to them – as indeed it did to the King himself: *»May this betrothal turn out to be more than a pious hope,«* Charlotte Leyden wrote to Ignaz von Döllinger in January 1867, expressing her reservations.

GROWING DOUBTS

There were early indications that Ludwig had not decided to marry Sophie out of love. For example, he forbade *»individual congratulations«,* stating that congratulations could be made at court balls instead.

He stayed only an hour at a ball held at the Bavarian Foreign Office in honour of his betrothal, attended by 750 guests, leaving to watch the end of a performance of Schiller's »Mary Stuart«. After the final curtain fell, he departed straight away for Berg Castle.

Ludwig travelled comparatively frequently during 1867. He and his brother Otto travelled to Eisenach at the beginning of June to visit the Wartburg, the setting of Wagner's opera »Tannhäuser«. The King wanted to see the real Wartburg in preparation for a new production of »Tannhäuser« in Munich. In July, the World Exhibition drew him to Paris. He would have liked to stay longer than a week, but the death of his uncle King Otto of Greece forced him to return to Munich sooner than planned.

Ludwig even intended to spend several weeks in Italy, although this did not take place for political reasons. Otherwise, as in previous years Ludwig enjoyed long riding excursions, mountain hikes and spending time in cabins in the

In January 1867, Duchess Sophie in Bavaria and King Ludwig II had several official photographs taken to mark the occasion of their betrothal.

mountains. He saw little of Sophie – and not for reasons of propriety, as might be expected.

No, this was not how a loving couple should appear. Even the official engagement photographs reveal the bride and bridegroom's inner detachment. On one of the shots they are even looking in different directions. This distance between them existed even though this was not an arranged union – on the contrary: it was based upon the King's free decision and probably upon loving affection on the part of the bride.

As he did so often, Ludwig used language to create an emotionally charged imaginary realm that did not exist in reality. He called his bride *»Elsa«* and himself *»Heinrich«* – after the German king who judges Elsa, Lohengrin's future bride, in the Lohengrin myth (and in Wagner's opera of the same name). Accordingly, Ludwig appears to have seen Sophie less as his bride and the future mother of his children – otherwise he would have had to refer to himself as the swan knight – and more as a subject whose fate he could decide.

Preparations for the wedding were already in full swing, even though no date had been set as yet. Commemorative leaflets and souvenirs with portraits of the couple went on sale, as did a medal; photographs of the two were sold everywhere. Ludwig had the rooms facing the court gardens in the Munich *Residenz* redecorated as living rooms and ceremonial chambers in the style of the French King Louis XV for his future queen, who turned 20 on 22 February 1867.

After weeks without a fixed date, public and family pressure grew too great, and the court determined that the wedding would be held on 12 October, the same day as Ludwig's grandparents (1810) and parents (1842) had married.

AWAKENED FROM DARK DREAMS

The King still showed no inclination to fulfil his promise to marry Sophie and had the date moved once again. Duchess Ludovika, the mother of the bride, voiced her annoyance towards the King's mother at the end of September 1867: *»You will understand that the delay to the wedding made me fearful and doubtful of the King's love for Sophie...* [Sophie has] *released him from his word in writing, but he has not accepted this.«* She added a few days later: *»This repeated deferral of the wedding has created an atmosphere unfavourable to us, and has given rise to such unpleasant talk that Max* [Sophie's father] *felt forced to write and tell the King that…he had to ask him most humbly to either abide by the date in the last days of November, or regard the request for Sophie's hand, which he made to us over eight months ago, as undone…«*

The King reacted extremely angrily to Duke Max's letter, as he regarded his future father-in-law as a subordinate for whom it was highly inappropriate to make such demands. Even though the date of the wedding had only just been moved officially to 29 November, Ludwig availed himself of the opportunity presented by Max's intervention. He wrote to Sophie on 7 October: *»I have now had time to examine and take counsel with myself, and I can now see that now, as before, my deep, passionate brotherly love for you is rooted deep in my soul, but not the kind of love that is needed for the union in marriage…*[it is] *better if we part from one another now and do not bind ourselves in the future through certain promises…«* By contrast, in his diary he wrote: *»Sophie is written off, the gloomy image is dissolving, I long for freedom, I thirst for freedom, as I revive after a tortuous nightmare.«*

Ludwig also told others about his broken engagement. While he admitted to Cosima von Bülow that he had given Sophie his trust, *»my friendship, but not love!«*, he wrote to Richard Wagner: *»That which occupied me over the last months, that which burdened me like a nightmare, tortured me terribly, you will have seen from my letters to our friend* [Cosima]*; now I feel so happy, I am able to breathe freely, I have awakened from dark dreams…«* Ludwig II made very similar statements in his letters to Sybilla von Leonrod: *»…there is no hurry for me at the moment; for I am young, and marrying in the near future would have been a premature step.«*

The public and, to an even greater degree, the Wittelsbach family reacted with displeasure to the King's decision, even though many had already seen it coming. Empress Elisabeth expressed herself in her characteristically open manner, here in a letter to her mother Ludovika: *»You can imagine how scandalised both I and the Emperor are by the King. There are no words for such behaviour. I simply cannot understand how he* *can show his face in Munich after everything that has happened. I am only glad that Sophie is taking it so well, God knows she would never have been able to be happy with such a man...«*

»Aunt Empress« – Ludwig's relationship with Elisabeth of Austria

»Aunt Empress arrived late in the evening,« Ludwig wrote to his cousin Wilhelm in faraway Darmstadt in 1862, keeping him up to date with events in Munich. This »aunt«, who arrived bearing presents for Ludwig and Otto as befitted an older relative, was none other than the Austrian Empress, Elisabeth of Austria (1837–1898), who was called Sisi or Lisi by her family.

Elisabeth was the daughter of Duke Maximilian in Bavaria's and eight years older than Ludwig, and had left Munich in 1854 as the bride of the Austrian Emperor Franz Joseph. While Ludwig and Elisabeth had known one another since childhood, closer contact between His Royal and Her Imperial Majesty only developed after Ludwig ascended the Bavarian throne. Their encounter in Bad Kissingen, where they both spent several weeks during the summer of 1864, contributed to their friendship. By then, Ludwig, now matured, and the young and beautiful Elisabeth really had something to say to one another. Both probably recognised that they had a similar view of people and the world in general. The relationship between Ludwig and Elisabeth is often referred to as a friendship between kindred spirits. But while certainly significant, it remained just that, a friendship.

The Bavarian King took every opportunity to prove himself a gentleman: he went to greet the Empress at Munich Station when she travelled through or arrived in the city (and did so even when he was ill), sent her bouquets of flowers on her frequent visits to Bavaria to see her family, accompanied her part of the way on train journeys and was happy when he could pay his

respects to her in person, mainly in Possenhofen or Feldafing. *»Yesterday the King paid me a long visit, and if grandmamma had not finally joined us, he would still be here. He kissed my hand so much that Aunt Sophie, who looked in through the door, asked me whether I still had it,«* Elisabeth wrote to her son Rudolf in March 1865. Ludwig told the Empress, whom he now called *»cousin«*, in 1867: *»The feeling of most sincere love and adoration and the most loyal devotion, which I already felt for you in my heart when I was still a boy, gives me a sense of heaven on earth and will only be extinguished by death.«* Despite their closeness, the Empress refused to permit Ludwig to visit her in Bad Ischl.
Elisabeth had reason to be very displeased with Ludwig. For one, she was annoyed that Bavaria had recognised the Kingdom of Italy in 1865 under international law. Not only had this young nation fought against Austria and annexed Austrian territory; the new state had also cost Elisabeth's sister Marie Sophie and her husband the crown of the Two Sicilies by conquering their kingdom. In addition, the Austrian Empress regarded the way Ludwig had behaved towards her sister Sophie in 1867 as completely scandalous.
In June 1881, both Sisi and Ludwig were staying on Lake Starnberg and thus saw one another frequently. At one of these meetings, Ludwig met Elisabeth's thirteen-year-old daughter Marie Valérie, who was allowed to give him a bouquet of jasmine blossom. In her diary, the girl described this encounter with the words: *»O! Fat King, now I have really given you my jasmine!«*, also adding that the King spoke quickly and indistinctly. A few days later, the Cabinet Secretary told a friend that the Empress had paid a return visit: *»...She arrived unexpectedly by boat with a moor. The King was startlingly charming and led her to the kiosk, the stables and so on, and accompanied her as far as Possenhofen in her boat, from whence he returned at nine in*

the evening, rowed by Hesselschwerdt.« Four years later, Elisabeth wrote a poem about this meeting and secreted it in a hiding place in the Casino on the *Roseninsel* known only to her and Ludwig. When the King discovered the greeting left by his like-minded friend, he wrote her an answer in verse and hid it in turn:

Thou eagle, aloft on the mountains,
From the lake and its waves below
To thee the gull sends greeting
Up, up to the eternal snow.

Once we encountered each other,
In the grey depths of time, on this mere,
With its mirroring calm, in the sweetness
Of roses, the spring of the year.

Side by side our boats silently glided,
Sunk in a stillness profound...
Barcarolles sung by a moor
In the stern was the only sound.

Elisabeth, 20 June 1885

The gull's salute from the distant strand
Reached the eagle's eyrie in mountain land,
On the gentle beat of its feathered limbs
It brought remembrance of olden times.

Eagle and gull both drifted that day
Into the enchanted, rose-scented bay,
And, boat meeting boat in majestic sweep,
They saluted each other across the deep.

Of the gull down on the shingly shore
Thinks the eagle up on the heights once more,
And his beating wings fond greetings bestow
From the peak mirrored in the lake below.

Ludwig, 11 September 1885

These verses and dates reveal that Ludwig and Sisi had not seen one other for some time. Nevertheless, the sense of closeness still remained. When the Empress heard of her cousin's death in Berg – she and her household were staying at Hotel Strauch in Feldafing (which today is called »Hotel Kaiserin Elisabeth«) on the lake's opposite shore – she mourned *»not only the sad end of a genial king, but also the death of a childhood friend,«* and was *»filled with pity and memories of happy hours and completely beside herself with grief«* (according to Marie Valérie). In Elisabeth's opinion, the King was *»no fool, only a misfit living in (other) worlds of ideas.«*

As a last greeting, the Empress sent to Munich a bouquet with jasmine blossom she herself had picked, which was placed in the dead King's right hand as he lay on his bier. Two days later, Elisabeth had mass said

for her friend in the village church in Feldafing and visited the Church of St. Michael in Munich herself to lay a wreath on the King's coffin.
Some of Elisabeth's poems, which only became known after her death, show the Empress trying to deal with her grief and pain. In them, she accuses Ludwig's successor, Prince Regent Luitpold, of stealing his throne: *»See the duplicitous old man! / Does his conscience not oppress him? / Folds his hands so piously, / his visage both sweet and sour.«*

SECRET LOVES

Surviving letters and documents reveal what Ludwig and Sophie's true feelings were during the time of their engagement. *»Why did I have to meet you, now that my freedom has been cast in chains?«* Sophie wrote on 23 July 1867 to Edgar Hanfstaengl. The son of the famous photographer Franz Hanfstaengl was in his father's studio when more engagement photographs were made. When he delivered the additional order of photographs to the ducal palace in the Ludwigstraße, Sophie fell in love with him. The secret relationship between the two lovers was doomed to fail from the beginning because of the difference in their social status. Sophie was wracked with guilt due to the promise she had given to Ludwig, who knew nothing of where Sophie's affections truly lay: *»I want to die in your arms and my name should fade – the world should forget that a Bavarian royal bride ever lived,«* she confided to Edgar Hanfstaengl.

However, Sophie was not the only one to have been mentally unfaithful during the time that she and Ludwig were betrothed. Ludwig likewise was much closer to another person: *»On that blessed sixth day of May 1867…*[we met], *never to part again, and never to leave one another until death,«* the King wrote to his close friend Richard Hornig in March 1872. Hornig was four years older than the King and (besides Karl Hesselschwerdt) was his closest companion and a kind of private secretary up until 1885. But he was also more than this: in Ludwig's diaries, he is often idolised as *»Richard, beloved of my soul…«*

Unlike her former fiancé, Sophie later married. In September 1868 she became the wife of Prince Ferdinand of Bourbon-Orléans, Duke of Alençon and grandson of King Louis Philippe of France, who had lost his throne in 1848. The wedding chorus from »Lohengrin« was played during the wedding ceremony. The previous evening Ludwig II had had a splendid firework display set off in Berg, on the other side of the lake; however, this was not done to mark the eve of his former bride's wedding, but as a present for Czarina Maria Alexandrovna, who was visiting him at the time. Ludwig was already back in his own, more acceptable world. He had previously admitted to Prince Wilhelm of Hesse: *»I find it very unpleasant to be completely surrounded by the family of my former bride.«* As time went by, his visits to Possenhofen became more frequent again, even though Ludwig's main reason was to see the Empress of Austria.

»O Prince! We faithfully beg of you: hear our plea! Give us a Queen!«, an anonymous author implored in 1879, encapsulating the sentiment of the Bavarian people. However, this wish was never to be granted, for after 1867 Ludwig II gave no more thought to marriage.

*»Either I rule or the people rule,
no good can come of both of us doing so.«*

7 Ludwig at a political crossroads

While everything was being prepared for the Bavarian royal wedding, the conflict between pro- and anti-Prussian forces was escalating both in parliament and in the public sphere. In August 1866, more than ninety percent of the members of parliament present had endorsed plans to unify the German states *»through closer ties with Prussia«*. The President of the Ministerial Council, Ludwig von der Pfordten, opposed the outcome of this non-binding vote and continued to press for a confederation of Southern German states with closer ties to Austria. However, during the course of the following months he lost his position and thus his chance to lead Bavaria and realise his plan.

Chlodwig zu Hohenlohe-Schillingsfürst, whom the King appointed at the end of December 1866 as von der Pfordten's successor, was well known for his pro-Prussian sentiment. He envisaged Bavaria becoming one federal state in a Germany dominated by Prussia. This obviously conflicted with the convictions held by the King, for whom nothing was of greater importance than maintaining the sovereignty of his country and his own royal station. However, in the light of Bavaria's weakened position and Prussia's strength, the appointment of a Prussia-friendly first minister was an important signal to the North that Bavaria was willing to compromise. The aim was to avoid unnecessary conflict and open up further political options.

NO ALTERNATIVES

Ludwig's decision to appoint Prince Hohenlohe met with bitter resistance among Ludwig's family and thus among the House of Imperial Councillors, which was dominated by the royal princes. The First House perceived a serious threat to Bavaria's independence. However, Ludwig was probably of the opinion that he would be able to curb his new President of the Ministerial Council and the latter's policies favouring German unification.

By contrast, the King's choice met with approval in the Second House, the *Landtag*, which at this point was dominated by liberal pro-Berlin forces. They were led by the *»Deutsche Fortschrittspartei in Bayern«* (the »German Progress Party in Bavaria«), which had been founded in 1863. Its party line, which demanded both greater powers for parliament and closer ties with Prussia, conflicted with the King's point of view.

In 1865, the Progress Party had already succeeded in decoupling the financial period from the *Landtag's* legislative period, shortening it to two years (which meant that the members of parliament had greater influence). In August 1867, some of the party's delegates demanded a reduction of the King's civil list, from which he financed all the costs for his royal household. Accordingly, the King was relieved when this attack on his finances was ultimately unsuccessful – but his dislike of the Progress Party grew, and he ordered that it be monitored more closely by the Home Office.

When attacks on Hohenlohe because of his Prussian-friendly policies became increasingly vehement, Ludwig began to doubt whether he had appointed the right person. He asked Duke Karl Theodor for his advice, who pointed out the options and rights of a regent in a letter of 29 March 1867: *»in a monarchist state it is unavoidable and necessary to show trust in one's minister, but conversely he should be closely supervised…after all, the minister is only supposed to be a tool in the hands of the King.«* This confirmed Ludwig's sceptical attitude towards Hohenlohe.

Under Hohenlohe, the German Customs Union was reformed on 8 July 1867 as an economic federation to which all individual German states belonged. Representatives of the Southern German states were included in the Federal Council and Federal Assembly of the North German Federation, thus creating a Customs Federal Council and Assembly. The

North German Confederation had been formed in 1866 as a military alliance, and in April 1867 became a federation of twenty-two states under Prussian supremacy. Bavaria had no alternative to cooperating with the politically influential Customs Union if damage to its economy was to be avoided.

However, this economic union was already a first step towards political union. Because of the loss of Bavarian sovereign powers and rights the treaty entailed, the First House only agreed to sign it after much resistance and the intervention of the King himself.

THE PATRIOTS' SUCCESS

The King was greatly changed by this political conflict and the personal troubles following the cancellation of his wedding: »*The K*[ing's] *condition (not physically) is really a cause for great concern. He has become increasingly rude and off-putting towards those around him,*« Döllinger reported to Charlotte Leyden on 26 October 1867. Indeed, the King's fears both for his future and for the future of his country increased, as he informed President of the Ministerial Council Hohenlohe towards the end of November 1867: »*I am extremely concerned about the independence of my crown and the autonomy of my country.*«

The first elections for the Customs Parliament on 10 February 1868 unexpectedly presented a further challenge. It was not the trade-friendly liberals that won a majority, but the candidates loyal to the King and above all to the Church. From now onwards, the conservative Catholic forces, which combined to form the »*Patriotenpartei*« or Patriots' Party, were to gain majorities in all elections.

Even though the anti-Prussian and monarchic line of the Patriots' Party was basically in the King's interests, and supported the system he preferred, it was at the same time loyal to the Pope, which Ludwig could in no way reconcile with his own views. He saw the Catholic clergy and its influence on people, society and politics as a rival to royal power and supremacy.

»The generation of steadfast character and spirit, the people of courage and right conviction that I want and need, they have all died out, one encounters only half-heartedness and half-measures, which is why I feel alone and abandoned on this earth, as someone left over from better days, transplanted into the present time, which I hate and in which I shall always feel alien.«

Ludwig II to Sybilla von Leonrod, Soiern, 16 September 1869

When the *Landtag* elections in the spring of 1869 resulted in a stalemate between the liberals and the patriots, new elections were called. With the King's approval, the ministers redrew the constituency boundaries to favour the liberals. Despite this manipulation, the decisive election in November 1869 was won by the Patriots' Party, which gained the majority of votes. The Patriots' success, which reversed the majorities that had existed in parliament up until then, was the result of voters' fear of the loss of national independence. At the same time, it was also a sign of protest against reforms in domestic policy – a protest that was also backed by the Catholic Church.

Even though Hohenlohe offered to resign in the light of the election results, the King kept him in office. His unlimited right to appoint ministers meant that he was able to appoint his ministers solely from the opposition, against the majority in the Second House – and thus also against the will of the electorate. This remained the case throughout his reign.

»The splendour of royalty!« – The cult surrounding the Bourbon dynasty

Ludwig was not only fascinated by medieval legends, an enthusiasm inspired mainly by the works of Richard Wagner; he also had a keen interest in the time of the French kings of the Bourbon dynasty of the 17th and 18th centuries, which was kindled by his *»good uncle«* Adalbert. These absolutist rulers based the legitimacy of their claim to the throne on their appoint-

Ludwig II in the costume of a Grand Master of the Bavarian House Order of the Knights of St George. This picture was commissioned by the King and was modelled upon the state portraits of 18th-century French kings. – Etching by Wilhelm Hecht, 1883.

ment to the royal office by God himself. This is referred to as the divine right of kings, or rule by divine right.
In 1866, Ludwig asked Richard Wagner what the meaning of the name »Lohengrin« was. The composer responded that the name could be translated as »sun countenance« (*Lohe* = light, fiery glow, *Grin* = face), which opened up yet another layer of significance to which Ludwig could relate. After all, King Louis XIV of France had taken the sun of the Greco-Roman God Apollo as his symbol.
Apollo stands for moral purity and temperance, and Ludwig had a similar view of Lohengrin as the incarnation of purity and Christian virtue. Accordingly, it was only a short (albeit decisive) step from the sun kingship of Louis XIV to the ideas and notions linked to the Holy Grail. An additional factor is that the sun god Apollo's holy animal, like Lohengrin's, is the swan – the epitome of grace and dignity. Ludwig II was thus able to connect the religious concept of the Grail with Bourbon rule.
As a member of the Wittelsbach family, it was not difficult for him to establish direct personal links with the French kings. His grandfather Ludwig I, at his christening in 1786 in Strasbourg, had been held in the arms of the last absolutist French King Louis XVI (the great-great-grandson of the sun king Louis XIV). Ludwig II believed that a sacred relationship ordained by fate between himself and the Bourbons had been established through his grandfather's baptism, and saw himself as standing in the line of the true kings *»of serene divine right«*. For the devout king, the sacrament of baptism both conferred grace and established identity. After all, in the 19th century it was more common to celebrate a person's name day than their birthday – for Ludwig, whose name day and birthday were one and the same, this date was a double celebration. He believed in the magic significance of names

and dates, and believed it was no coincidence that he not only bore the same name as the French kings but was also born on the holy day of the Louis IX of France, who had been declared a saint. Louis IX was not only one of the most important medieval European monarchs (often regarded as the ideal type of the Christian ruler), he was also an ancestor of the Bourbons. This explains why Ludwig II always surrounded himself with images of his »ancestor« and sainted namesake Louis IX and insisted that the image of his »patron« be used to decorate sacred spaces.
From 1867 onwards, Ludwig studied the history and significance of the Bourbons more closely. In his diary, he noted: *»Read about Louis XIV, the power of the ruler, a time of the flowering, the splendour of kingship; omnipotence, the glory of majesty, royal divinity«* and *»increase in the feeling of being a king.«* On 12 August 1869, Ignaz von Döllinger reported to his friend that Ludwig had ordered books on France and the Bourbons *»by the hundredweight«*. The King was a passionate reader, who also requested and was sent rare and secret literature, and over the years became a specialist in this epoch of French history, which was of course made easier by his excellent knowledge of French.
In his diary, entries alternate between German and French, and Ludwig liked to sign these entries as *»Louis le Roi«* and *»Roi de Bavière«*. For him, the French kings from Louis XIV to Louis XVI were more than mere role models. They were a significant influence on his life. For example, the Bavarian King held funeral masses for both Louis XVI and his wife Marie Antoinette every year on the day of their execution. Cabinet Secretary Friedrich von Ziegler wrote to Ludwig's Court Secretary about this tradition on 21 January 1882: *»Today was the funeral mass for Louis XIV. The mood here is miserable...«* For Ludwig, these rulers became his intercessors and protectors. For instance,

he noted in his diary: »*On 21 January, the day of the murder of King Louis XVI, a day that is forever dark and terrible, a funeral mass, I vowed once again before the image of the Holy Virgin and the Christ Child and before the image of Holy King Louis IX…also vowing before the image of King Louis XIV the Great to overcome evil…*«
Apart from Switzerland, France was the only non-German country that the King travelled to: in 1867, 1874 and 1875 he visited the most important locations associated with Bourbon rule, including Versailles Palace in 1875 and Reims Cathedral, where the French kings were crowned. It was here, in this sacred place, on 25 August 1875 – his birthday and name day – that he invoked his patron saint and his royal protectors beneath the cathedral's Gothic vaulting as he completed his thirtieth year.

A LACK OF SELF-CONFIDENCE

Ludwig's appointment of liberal ministers at first seems hard to understand, but it can be explained not only by his marked aversion to political Catholicism loyal to Rome, but also by his own idiosyncratic understanding of the royal office. The Patriots could have become his closest allies in the preservation of Bavaria's rights as a sovereign state. However, for Ludwig any consideration of the parliamentary majority when forming a government was tantamount to a weakening of the monarchic principle. He refused to submit to the will of the people and wanted to be the one who decided matters himself. In this regard, Ludwig II was just as autocratic as his grandfather Ludwig I. He informed his Cabinet Secretary: »*The crown must ensure the well-being of the people, but it must not share Its holy rights with Its mutinous subjects, who are devoid of any submissiveness, any obedience…Either I rule or the people rule, no good can come of both of us doing so.*«

This attitude expressed a misunderstanding on Ludwig's part as well as a lack of self-confidence. He did not comprehend that the power and efficacy of a 19th-century monarch depended on the extent to which he or she was accepted and loved by his or her people. By treating the will of the people with contempt, he created a rift between himself and his real power base that became impossible to bridge. Furthermore, the idea of the monarchy became ever weaker the more the King refused to show himself in person and demonstrate his strength in public. Even though he feared that the Catholic Church, the Patriots' Party and parliamentarianism would weaken the crown, he failed to take the only right step – which would have been to react flexibly and openly to the changes of his time, thus keeping the idea of the monarchy alive and preserving it for the future.

The years from 1867 to 1869 under Hohenlohe were also a time of reform. First ideas for these reforms had already been developed under Maximilian II, and now they could finally be implemented. The »Homeland, Marriage and Residency Act« not only gave the people greater freedom to travel and trade, but also made it possible for citizens with no recognised religion to marry in civil ceremonies. A new municipal code expanded local government, a new army constitution ensured fair military service (every male Bavarian citizen had to serve for three years in the active forces, for three years in the reserve forces, and for five years in the territorial army), and the »Act concerning Public Poor Relief and Healthcare« improved social welfare.

Bavaria was better prepared for the future than it ever had been – but this future was to bring the end of Bavarian independence.

»May God preserve us from the claws of Prussia«

8 1870/71 and its consequences

Nothing precipitated Ludwig II's final withdrawal from public life and active politics so much as the events of 1870 and 1871. The Franco-Prussian War and the foundation of the German Reich under Prussian supremacy marked an even greater turning point in the Bavarian king's life than his geographical separation from Richard Wagner.

Many years previously, Ludwig had made it clear to those close to him how low his regard was for his mother's native country and the militarism it prized so highly. Towards the end of 1867, he wrote to his confidante Sybilla von Leonrod: *»May God preserve us from the claws of Prussia: O, these are grave, grave times!«*

In spite of his mistrust of Prussia, the King complied with the advice of his President of the Ministerial Council and pursued policies aimed at German unification. Nevertheless, with a last gleam of hope, he asked Hohenlohe in the summer of 1869 whether the alliance of protection and defence between Bavaria and Prussia could not be terminated. However, this was not possible – neither in legal nor in political terms.

Ludwig's dislike of all things Prussian was revealed in exemplary fashion in his reaction to an event that would have left a more confident monarch unaffected: the poet Emanuel Geibel, who was born in Lübeck but had been granted a Bavarian honorary professorship in German literature and poetry and received an annual stipend, wrote a laudatory poem in honour of King Wilhelm I of Prussia's visit to Geibel's home town in September 1868. The poem ended by expressing the wish that the Prussian king would see *»how your eagle flies across the entire Reich / from the mountains to the sea.«* Ludwig II was affronted that an artist paid from his cabinet treasury should speak out in favour of the unification of all German states under Prussia in this way. The King had Geibel's stipend cancelled immediately.

The contradiction between the King's personal inclinations and his political conduct became particularly evident towards the end of 1869, when Ludwig refused to accept in person a document formulated by the House of Imperial Councillors, which contained a vote of no confidence in the entire ministry under Hohenlohe. »*The people know very well how audiences are granted to various personages from the theatre etc., and thus condemn all the more strongly the fact that the Imperial Councillors' deputation was not received,*« a newspaper wrote, expressing its inability to understand the King's decision. While the conservative forces' rejection of unification-focused policies actually reflected the King's own intentions, Ludwig forbade any kind of criticism of his policies, especially an intervention of the First House in the form of a written statement.

DWINDLING AUTHORITY

During these months of extreme political tension, Ludwig was conscious of the need to address the representatives of the new *Landtag* with a King's speech in the throne room of the *Residenz*: »*I know that some of your hearts are filled with concern that Bavaria's rightful independence is threatened. This fear is groundless...as much as I long and hope for the restoration of a national alliance of German states, I will only consent to a Germany in which Bavaria's independence is not put at risk.*« Ludwig opened the *Landtag* on 17 January 1870 with these words, which had been penned by Minister Hohenlohe. Reactions to this speech were muted, as Ludwig's words did not seem to correspond to political reality.

The situation was not improved by opinions such as those voiced for example by the newspaper »Bayerisches Vaterland« (»Bavarian Fatherland«) in its edition of 1 February: *»We are Bavarian patriots, and as such we know that it is our duty to honour the King, but we live in a century in which the people have their own rights, even towards kings. Furthermore,* *in this regard the Bavarian people are entitled to even greater rights than any other.«*

These words came from the particularly radical wing of the Patriots' Party. This wing united the so-called »Ultramontanists«, that is, those who felt their first duty was to the Curia in Rome »over the mountains« (Latin *ultra montes* – the mountains refer to the Alps).

Other interested parties among the higher-ranking officials played upon Ludwig's fear of the Ultramontanists, hoping to weaken his dislike of the Progress Party. And indeed, by now the King was convinced that the Ultramontanists posed a greater threat to the throne and state than the progressives.

Anti-Prussian countries observed the proceedings in Bavaria with great concern. The »Wiener Freie Presse« wrote: *»Today, only a monarch of ruthless, inflexible willpower can act in opposition to the determined will of the people. Such a line of action, however, is always a great misfortune for the country, and may also under certain circumstances be a threat to the throne.«*

The First and Second Houses' unanimous rejection of Hohenlohe and his policies reveals just how much the King's authority had suffered. In the end, the King was unable to withstand this united front, despite his desire to keep Hohenlohe in office. On 7 March 1870 Ludwig accepted Hohenlohe's resignation and appointed as his successor the independent Otto von Bray-Steinburg. As mentioned above, it went against Ludwig's understanding of kingship to go along with the majority faction in the Second House and choose a President of the Ministerial Council from the ranks of the Patriots. This would have been tantamount to giving up his most powerful political right, the right to appoint ministers.

While Bray-Steinburg was less enthusiastic about the issue of German unification than his predecessor Hohenlohe, he nevertheless regarded the Customs Union Treaty and the protection and defence alliance with Prussia of 1866 as unavoidable.

CONFRONTATION WITH FRANCE

In the summer of 1870, the virulent conflict between Prussia and France was nearing its climax. A prince from the Sigmaringen branch of the Hohenzollern dynasty which ruled Prussia was standing as a candidate for the vacant Spanish throne. The French feared encirclement by enemy forces and demanded that the Hohenzollern prince withdraw his candidacy. Although the Hohenzollern family complied with this demand, the sabre-rattling on either side of the Rhine continued. France, ruled by Napoleon III, insisted on wider-reaching guarantees, for reasons of domestic policy: King Wilhelm I of Prussia, as head of the Hohenzollern dynasty, was to promise that in future, no member of his family would claim the Spanish throne. Wilhelm I rejected this request, however. Bismarck subsequently produced a curt message (the »Ems Dispatch«) transmitting his King's reaction, which was intentionally leaked to the public and led to calls for retribution amongst the French population. This French national outrage was exactly the result the Prussian Prime Minister had envisaged. His aim was to instigate a war, so as to promote German unification through conflict with a foreign power.

On the same day the French learned of the dispatch, the Bavarian Minister of War Siegmund von Pranckh promised to place the Bavarian army at Prussia's disposal according to the terms of the protection and defence alliance, should France declare war. This was done without consulting either Bray-Steinburg or Ludwig II.

At the same time, the Bavarian diplomats were promoting peace negotiations mediated by the English government. Ludwig, who had returned to Berg Castle from a trip to the mountains because of the tense situation, also *»repeatedly expressed his keen wish that a peaceful solution be found to the conflict,«* as his Cabinet Secretary August von Eisenhart noted. *»Hours passed in discussions about the controversial state of affairs, in weighing up the circumstances,...the King once more demonstrated his characteristic ability to grasp things* *clearly and speedily...the question* [was] *debated whether Bavaria could remain neutral, or whether it would be forced to fight at Prussia's side according to the alliance treaty of 1866.«*

THE EUPHORIA OF WAR

The King did not take the decision to mobilise his armies lightly and sought advice from all sides. Ultimately, however, he had only one choice: to recognise the *casus foederis* and sign the mobilisation order prepared by Bray-Steinburg on behalf of all ministers. Ludwig also travelled to Munich, although he hated the city vehemently by now. Large crowds gathered in front of the *Residenz*, greeting the monarch enthusiastically when he appeared at an open window. On the whole, the population was satisfied with the King's quick and clear decision.

A few days later – France had officially declared war upon Prussia in the meantime – large groups of people returned to the royal residence, celebrating Ludwig with patriotic songs such as »Die Wacht am Rhein« (»The Watch by the Rhine«).

The Second House and its members of parliament were unable to stand on one side in the overheated atmosphere and recognised the alliance with Prussia by authorising the war expenditure. The parliamentary debate split the Patriots' Party, whose delegates were unable to agree on the right course of action. This weakened the party decisively for many months.

On 27 July, as the Prussian Crown Prince Friedrich Wilhelm came to take command of the Bavarian army under the terms of the treaty, Prussian flags were raised in Munich. Ludwig wrote the Crown Prince a letter, expressing his ideas for the future: *»I believe I can assume from the enlightened insight of Your noble father, the King I revere so greatly, that it is also his will that Bavaria's integrity as a state – unlike the German nationalist course – will emerge from that conflict unscathed and be preserved henceforth.«*

This was the King's hope. The reality of the situation was very different, and the success in battle of the 55,000 Bav-

At the end of July 1870, Ludwig II welcomes Crown Prince Friedrich Wilhelm at Munich Central Station and accompanies him to the Residenz, cheered by the people. – Wood engraving based on a drawing by Ludwig Bechstein, 1870.

arian (and other South German) soldiers in the brutal and terrible war contributed significantly to this. News of repeated victories fanned the people's desire for national unity – exactly as Bismarck had foreseen. After the decisive battle at Sedan on 1 September 1870 and capture of the French Emperor Napoleon III, there was no stopping it.

CLINGING TO SYMBOLS

One person refused to take part in the celebrations: »*...the fact that the monarch remained absent, that he scorned to pay homage displeased the public,*« wrote one of the King's contemporary biographers. Ludwig was angry that Prussian flags had been raised in Munich and insisted on symbols of Bavarian sovereignty. Thus he instructed Eisenhart on 3 September: »*...As there is no German Empire, no German republic, no German Federation so far, and the so-called German colours in reality are the colours of a geographical concept, I want only Bavarian flags, or even better, no flags to be raised above governmental buildings...*«

Ludwig's clinging to the symbols of Bavarian independence had long become futile. More and more Bavarians were demanding a unified state with a *Kaiser* (Emperor) at its head, and more and more Bavarian towns were sending the King petitions to join a unified Germany. In a memorandum, the ministers in their entirety requested him to take action on the »German question«. The ministers were not in favour of joining the North German Confederation, however; they were hoping for a kind of confederacy of states.

THE GERMAN QUESTION

Opinions in the newspapers were divided. Some voices longed for the day that »*the greatest German prince of the South will offer the greatest German prince of the North his brotherly hand and give to the people what the people are due.*« Others reminded their readers that the King had stressed he »*would do nothing unworthy of his dignity as the heir and successor to many famous and noble princes, nothing unworthy of the prince and leader of a people with a history of a thousand years,*« that is, he would never permit Bavaria to be incorporated into a German Empire.

However, after Johannes Huber, the professor with whom he had enjoyed many discussions in 1864/65, also asked him to be proactive and »*offer the King of Prussia the crown of the German Empire,*« Ludwig realised that there was only one viable solution, from a political and economic perspective: »*The horrible thing about this dreadful matter is that Saxony and the princes of the other German states are to be enticed into making this offer if I refuse...to play this degrading role; if I do not do it, then they are perfidious enough to refuse to grant me, out of petty revenge, the small concessions that Prussia is morally obliged to make,*« he wrote to Prince Luitpold, who – like most members of the Wittelsbach family – opposed the idea of a German Empire.

Ludwig saw the inevitable movement towards unification as a threat and spoke increasingly of abdication. He ordered his brother Otto, who was at the German headquarters in Versailles, to return to Bavaria, so they could discuss handing over the crown. Otto's unstable mental condition made it impossible for Ludwig to abdicate in favour of his brother, however, and sent the King into even greater depression.

In the meantime, Baden and Hesse-Darmstadt had agreed to join the North German Confederation. The Bavarian negotiator Bray-Steinburg continued to discuss only an extended federation with Bismarck, however, not a closer union in the form of a unified nation state. Bismarck thereupon threatened to isolate Bavaria. When it became known that the Kingdom of Württemberg also wanted to join the North German Confederation, the Bavarian negotiator changed his strategy. He was now prepared to discuss Bavaria's joining the Confederation under the terms of the North German Federal Constitution and granting the leader of the resulting federation the title of emperor. Bray-Steinburg did not ask the King's permission to do this. In general, Ludwig was given only little or late information on the respective status of negotiations, something he complained about regularly without achieving any real change.

TURNING POINT

The »Treaties of Versailles« of 23 November 1870, in which Bavaria bound itself to an *»eternal alliance«* with the North German Confederation and thus to the foundation of the German Reich, meant that Bavaria as it had existed up to that point was consigned to history; the country's independence was restricted and Ludwig II's sovereignty became a thing of the past.

Ludwig ratified the treaties on 7 December, as his country was granted both symbolic and actual privileges. While these concessions did not include the additional territory hoped for (especially a corridor to the exclave of the Rhenish Palatinate), it did contain »reserved and special rights« for Bavaria, including military sovereignty in time of peace, the right to its own railway system, the independence of its postal and telegraph system for the most part, the right to determine its own taxation on beer and spirits, the vice-presidency in the Federal Council and the diplomatic right to have its own foreign ambassadors. Ludwig defended these marks of Bavaria's special position staunchly for the remainder of his reign. *»I wish that it would have been possible to bring the federative principle to bear more strongly in the Federal Constitution; however, I will not refuse to grant my authorisation to the agreements in question because of this...«*, Ludwig wrote as a preface to his ratification – even though he was forced to accept restrictions of his military sovereignty, which was to him (the most unmilitary of kings!) one of the most important aspects of sovereignty.

From now on, and against better knowledge, the words published in the »Allgemeine Zeitung« became the official credo of the German Reich: *»King Ludwig of Bavaria has thus crowned the efforts he has made in the matter of Germany so far; he has given the House of Wittelsbach and the country of Bavaria an immortal place in history.«* This referred to the fact that Ludwig II, as the most important federal prince after the King of Prussia, in the name of all the other German states, offered the said King the title of German Kaiser in a letter (the »Kaiser letter«). Bismarck's plan had succeeded. He wanted and needed the offer of the title of Kaiser to Wilhelm I to come from someone of the same rank and not from the people. After all, at this point Bismarck's master was still unsure whether he actually wanted the title of Kaiser. An offer from the second most important German monarch, Ludwig II of Bavaria, was important in gaining Wilhelm's consent.

CROWNING THE KAISER

Many hurdles needed to be overcome before Ludwig II's »Kaiser letter« could be presented to his uncle Wilhelm I, however. The fact that Ludwig was able to offer the rank of emperor to King Wilhelm in a letter and was thus spared meeting him face to face in Versailles meant that at least one significant obstacle was removed. Under no circumstances did Ludwig want to offer the title in person – an act he regarded as a humiliation –, and he certainly did not want to do it in the palace of the French Bourbon kings he revered so greatly.

While Ludwig explained to his brother Otto that offering the rank of Kaiser was *»a politically prudent act, necessary in the interests of the crown and the country«*, Otto wrote on 28 November 1870 from Versailles: *»…I beg of you, do not do this terrible thing! How can there be any power that forces a lord and king to give up his independence and recognise any power above himself other than God!«* Otto's view was shared by most of the Wittelsbach family.

On 30 November, Maximilian von Holnstein arrived at Hohenschwangau. He had played a decisive role in the discussions and negotiations with the ministers Ludwig had sent to Versailles. In his pocket, the crown equerry carried a draft of the »Kaiser letter« written by Bismarck, which had been read, approved and slightly adapted by Bray-Steinburg on the train journey to Bavaria.

At Hohenschwangau, where Ludwig had been staying since the beginning of the month, the King refused to see the emissary for several hours, claiming he was suffering from toothache. Only when Holnstein put him under pressure by pointing out the possible risks of his failing to act did Ludwig sit down at his desk and copy Bismarck's draft as revised by the Minister of State, making a few small changes, in which Wilhelm I was offered *»the exercise of the rights of president of the federation and the right to carry the title of German Emperor«*.

Ludwig did not want to take all responsibility upon himself, however, and placed the ultimate decision in the hands of his Cabinet Secretary Eisenhart. Holnstein, who travelled to Munich the same evening, handed Eisenhart an accompanying note from the King, which read: »*...if the sacrifices...demanded of me are too great...then this matter fails, and I give you the authority to tear up the letter to the King of Prussia...I place the matter in your hands.*« On 3 December, Prince Luitpold, as Ludwig's representative, gave the »Kaiser letter« to Wilhelm I in Versailles.

There was now no going back, although three days later Ludwig sent a telegram to his Minister Johann von Lutz in Versailles, stating: »*If possible, Emperor should not be included in the constitution or only as a title, namely Emperor in Germany,*« and proposing unsuccessfully that the position of Kaiser should alternate between the Wittelsbach and the Hohenzollern families.

***»I hope that I will be rid of my fever, toe infection and catarrh for a long time to come«* – Ludwig, always ailing**

From childhood onwards, Ludwig II's freedom of action and movement was restricted by numerous ailments. Besides common illnesses such as the pox (1861) and measles (1862), which were quite dangerous in the 19th century, Ludwig was plagued by poor health, with sore throats and infections of the respiratory tract, which sometimes confined him to his chamber for months on end. As an adolescent, he also complained frequently of headaches and toothaches.

For example, on 16 March 1862 Ludwig wrote to his cousin Wilhelm of Hesse: »Today I have to start drinking whey because of my throat. On Saturday I will also inhale steam for my throat.« His correspondence with Sybilla von Leonrod also provides much information on the many times in Ludwig's life that illness restricted his activities.

He became bad-tempered when he could not ride, go on walks or drive out in his carriage for longer periods of time, as was the case in 1868. »I was forced to remain inside for several months owing to prolonged ill health. The day before yesterday was the first time I was able to drive out again, which was extremely pleasant, and I hope that I will be rid of my fever, toe infection and catarrh for a long time to come,« Ludwig wrote to his Hessian cousin with cautious optimism in April 1868.

Ludwig attributed this susceptibility to illness to his rapid growth as a child, and it made him exceedingly cautious. It is known that he often had enquiries made as to the health of persons he wished to visit.

From boyhood onwards, Ludwig II was troubled with severe toothache caused by periodontitis and plaque. The King was as neglectful of his teeth as he was attentive to the hygiene of the rest of his body. As a result, he started to lose his teeth quite early. In 1870, the Prussian Crown Prince Ludwig Wilhelm noticed that »Most of [Ludwig's] good looks have vanished, he has lost his front teeth.« Three years later, the writer Felix Dahn noted at an audience with Ludwig that »... when he spoke, several missing teeth disfigured his appearance and made it even more difficult to understand his words, which he sputtered out hastily.«

Even though the King was afraid of dentists and did not like them near him, he needed them urgently. He complained regularly to his servants about the dentists' rudeness, and was constantly on the lookout for new and better doctors, even abroad – without success.

»It is very important to me that you tell [court dentist] Prf. Koch that I...need him urgently, that his thing is not keeping at all and is a great bother to me; he should finally make it so it is definitely of use...«, Ludwig complained to a confidant about lost fillings and a removable partial denture made of rubber that was supposed to enable him to speak normally.

Ludwig's dental problems determined the sort of meals prepared for him, as one of his cooks recorded in his memoirs: »The King's tooth problems were well known to all of us in the kitchen. We had to adjust the cooking time so that all dishes, especially meat, were very soft, there were a lot of hashed dishes, omelettes, mash and so on; croustades or English roast meat, such as roast beef, steaks and so on were never allowed to be served.«

Although he knew that sweets and sweet wines were not good for him, Ludwig II gave up neither. A dentist reported that in February 1884, as soon as his dental treatment was over, the King had served a tray »of soft sponge cakes, little cream cakes, chocolates and a small bottle of sweet liqueur.«

During the last years of his life, his toothache was so severe that he often resorted to narcotics. When the King died at forty, the autopsy report stated that his upper jaw was »nearly toothless«, while »the lower jaw still [contained] a number of loose teeth (4 incisors and 2 canines) «.

Ludwig II suffered from extreme halitosis because of these dental problems. In order to spare those around him, he would sometimes hold a perfumed handkerchief in front of his mouth. The King's frequent bad temper with himself and others is completely understandable under these circumstances, and his physical decay increased the distance at which he kept the public. Incidentally, this particular ailment was one that Ludwig shared with his revered role model Louis XIV of France, who had lost all of his teeth by the age of forty. Ludwig was aware of this, for at one point he asked one of his dentists whether the French king had worn an artificial set of teeth; the dentist was forced to answer in the negative.

On 18 January 1871 the King of Prussia was declared the German Kaiser in the Hall of Mirrors in Versailles. Ludwig did not attend this historic event, which he felt to be a humiliation. The King of Württemberg, who was wracked with guilt over his country's dead and wounded soldiers, was also absent.

»O Ludwig, I cannot describe how infinitely pained and grieved I was during that ceremony, how every fibre of my being struggled and revolted against what I saw…What a sad impression it made upon me to see our Bavarians bowing to the Kaiser…everything so cold, so proud, so splendid, so magnificent and ostentatious and heartless and empty,« Otto wrote to his brother.

The House of the Imperial Councillors had approved the Treaties of Versailles, which required changes to the constitution, on 30 December 1870. However, the decision of the Second House was still pending. After some resistance, especially on the part of the Patriots, the vote took place three days after Wilhelm was proclaimed Kaiser (which had of course created a *fait accompli*); the Treaties were approved with two votes more than the required two-thirds majority. The King had contributed actively to this positive result. A few days before the decisive meeting of the *Landtag*, he made a point of thanking the Archbishop of Munich-Freising, a member of the First House, for his pro-Reich vote. In doing so, Ludwig hoped to weaken the Patriots' religious grounds for rejecting the Treaties.

»The coalition must take control of the entire country, like a terrible inquisition« – Plans for a secret society

The results of the 1866 war led Ludwig II to search for ways to strengthen the monarchy and his position as king – both in symbolic and in actual terms. From 1869 onwards his thoughts were occupied with plans to found a secret society, which he named »coalition«, in order to rescind the Constitution and introduce an absolutist system of government in Bavaria.

»The greater the king's power, the better he is able to act for the benefit of his people,« Ludwig wrote in 1869, noting down the principles of his own understanding of rulership.

As a first step, Ludwig asked Senior Lieutenant Wilhelm Reisenegger to create a kind of security force, which was to recruit mainly officers. The King saw the military as a possible ally in his secret plans for a *coup d'état*. This also explains why he attended a comparatively high number of appointments with his army and officers in the spring of 1870 and was more frequently seen in uniform – contrary to his usual habits. However, the »coalition« remained mere wishful thinking. It was only when Johann Krahl took charge after the founding of the Reich in 1871 that the plans for this secret society took on more concrete shape. »*The coalition must take control of the entire country, invisible but doubly powerful, like an unyielding, strict, terrible inquisition, nipping any stirrings of wickedness in the bud, and combatting both the liberal, democratic, nationalist and the ultramontanist Roman movement,*« Ludwig demanded in August 1871. He wanted unwelcome journalists, members of parliament, societies, parties and even members of his family to be intimidated. According to his plans, civilians were to organise themselves in »clubs« and thus support the »coalition«.

However, these plans – which the King pursued only half-heartedly – were to remain unsuccessful. During the 1870s, Ludwig brought them up again and again, in a less radical form than in 1871, but around 1880 he finally lost the energy for pursuing his plans for a secret society.

WAS THE IMPERIAL CROWN BOUGHT?

From 25 September 1873 to 1886, a total of five million marks was transferred from Swiss bank accounts to the Bavarian court treasury – and was thus directly available to the King. This money came from Otto von Bismarck's secret funds. Maximilian von Holnstein received ten per cent of this sum. It has been repeatedly speculated that Ludwig II's agreement to Bavaria's accession to the North German Confederation and to the »Kaiser letter« (where Holnstein acted as an intermediary) were bought – leading to the question of whether the Bavarian king was corrupt.

Besides the financial transactions, of which there is hard evidence, we also know that Cabinet Secretary Eisenhart conveyed Ludwig's financial requests to Minister Bray-Steinburg, who was conducting negotiations in Versailles: *»His Majesty the King has repeatedly instructed me to tell Your Excellency that He lives in the fond hope that Your Excellency will succeed in procuring 2 million for His Majesty.«*

The Bavarian ruler was not alone in his anticipation of financial compensation; many statesmen and military personnel expected favours in return for their political, military or other support of the creation of the German Reich – favours which were usually granted. In addition, the German countries received monies from the extremely high French reparation payments, which created a surplus in many national budgets – including Bavaria's. These payments were public knowledge.

In contrast, the payments made to Ludwig personally were kept secret, which at first sight makes his role in the foundation of the Reich appear suspicious. However, this view is inaccurate. In the first instance, all of the King's decisions followed the only route open to him in political terms. The alternative would have been to isolate Bavaria completely, cutting it off from the supply of Prussian coal and iron its industry depended upon.

Secondly, when Ludwig wrote the »Kaiser letter« and ratified the Treaties of Versailles, he did not know whether Bismarck would grant him the money he hoped for. The Prussian Prime Minister did not respond to the King's wishes at first, stating that it would be necessary to wait until peace negotiations were conducted with France (which only occurred well into 1871). Accordingly, Ludwig II made all of his decisions without any agreement on Bismarck's part to provide him with money. Ludwig considered the payments his due, given the sacrifices he was required to make. Thus, the most that can be said is that he was in the position of creditor. This advantage was so controversial, however, that it would have damaged Ludwig's reputation enormously had it become public knowledge – especially as the King had obviously been directly influenced by Prussia. In his turn, Bismarck was keen to secure Ludwig's favour and ensured he received a personal sign of thanks for his services.

HUMILITY AND RESPONSIBILITY

Writing retrospectively, Ludwig explained the reasons for his decision in a letter to Sybilla von Leonrod on 24 March 1871: *»It was in Bavaria's interests that I acted as I did, for if I had not made these sacrifices, which were so heavy both for the crown and for the country, sooner or later we would have been forced into much greater, much more painful things, without being able to preserve a semblance of volition, and this would have ruined our entire political future, as well as our position in the new Reich.«* Indeed, there had been no alternative for the King, and accordingly none for Bavaria. Ludwig made the only possible choice, acting as a responsible ruler with a clear understanding of what was at stake. The fact that his personal feelings and his innermost yearnings went in a completely different direction only serves to emphasise the drama of the times and explains why Ludwig withdrew into a kind of inner emigration as a result of the events of 1870/71.

9 Ludwig's most difficult struggle

»To be so utterly, utterly and completely alone in the desolate, dreary world, alone in my convictions, misunderstood and distrusted, that is no small matter,« Ludwig lamented to Richard Wagner in October 1869. And indeed, throughout his life the King had no one of more or less equal standing to support him in word and deed, in reciprocal trust and understanding. Even Wagner, who was thirty-two years older than the King, was unable to fill this role. Ludwig's loneliness was partly due to his position as monarch – but was more the result of the way he dealt with this position. Very few people were able to live up to his standards and expectations, either because they lacked intellectual profundity, because they did not understand his attitude to life or because they crossed the thin line between familiarity and deference to him, appointed by God, as Ludwig saw it. The separation anxiety resulting from the sudden loss of his wet nurse as a baby troubled him throughout his life. This was the reason he maintained a lifelong correspondence with Sybilla von Leonrod: *»You understand me so well, and apart from you so few do, so many misunderstood and continue to misunderstand me, so that I naturally felt more and more rejected by the world and withdrew into myself,«* he confessed to her in August 1872.

In April 1863 he told her about his recent friendship with Duke Karl Theodor in Bavaria, who was six years his senior: *»O, it is so wonderful to have a faithful, beloved friend, to whom one can cling amid the storms of life…« – »This poor soul is hated and misunderstood by almost everyone, but I know him better…«*, the Crown Prince wrote. This close contact lasted no more than four years, however.

WONDERFUL FRIEND

About the same time, Ludwig struck up an unusual friendship that was even closer than his bond with Karl Theodor and was marked by deep emotions. This attachment began in Berchtesgaden in the summer of 1863. *»Recently the two new ordinary officers visited us...*[one of whom was] *Lieutenant Prince Paul von Thurn und Taxis of the Second Artillery Regiment,«* Otto wrote to his cousin Wilhelm in Darmstadt on 17 May 1863. Otto had no inkling how important this soldier, born in 1843 into the highest ranks of the aristocracy, would become to his brother in the three years that followed. Ludwig and Paul shared a passion for the works of Wagner (especially »Lohengrin«) and for theatre in general.

The letters the two exchanged are of well-nigh unsurpassable effusiveness. Those surviving from 1866 seem strange for a friendship between two men, especially almost 150 years later. This is how Paul – who became the King's aide-de-camp in January 1865 – described their relationship in a letter to Ludwig: *»Now our friendship is completely different. Before, we were simply young, on the brink of adulthood, now it is a relationship between men...You reign supreme in my thoughts. You are everything to me.«* Other passages are in a similar vein: *»I press you to my heart in my thoughts«* , *»I had tears in my eyes when you left. O, Ludwig, Ludwig, I love you so!«*, *»My heart pounded when I passed the Residenz and saw there was still light in your window«* and *»You will be in my dreams, your comely face, your beautiful, loving eyes will gaze upon me...think of your Paul, who loves you.«* The wording suggests that the two men were in love. This may indeed have been the case, but a correct evaluation of the texts demands that the contemporary style of writing, Ludwig's emotional mode of expression, which his partners tried to match (as we saw in the case of Richard Wagner!), and an unusually effusive nature be taken into account.

Their relationship was by no means free of conflict, and Paul of Thurn and Taxis was repeatedly forced to evoke the feelings they shared: *»Yes, my dear friend, our relationship holds something noble together, it is no common friendship. We were brought together and united by a higher power!«* This confidant played a decisive role in preventing Ludwig from abdicating in July 1866: *»Your decision hit me hard, especially the lightness with which you are prepared to take this terribly serious step, which will destroy the great plans of you, your friends and ultimately all of us…O Ludwig, you are destined to do great things, but you will only be able to achieve them in your current position.«*

»You reign supreme in my thoughts. You are everything to me,« Paul von Thurn und Taxis described his unusual, emotionally charged friendship with Ludwig. Portrait photograph, c. 1862.

Paul von Thurn und Taxis had *»become presumptuous«*, Ludwig wrote to Sophie, his later fiancée, explaining why he had fired his closest companion as aide-de-camp in November 1866. The nobleman had fallen in love with a soubrette at the Munich *Volkstheater* (People's Theatre) and later married her. Paul was disowned and disinherited by his family for this; he was forced to give up the name »Thurn und Taxis«. He died in Cannes in 1879 as »Paul von Fels« (Ludwig later granted him a personal title). Without question, the music-loving Paul was the King's only close friend.

As had been the case with Karl Theodor previously, Ludwig was unable to get over the fact that Paul had fallen in love with a woman – and even married her. The King reacted similarly in his later relationships with men.

»ANNOYING FEMALES«

There were speculations about Ludwig's sexual orientation even during his lifetime. This would be of little interest to us today if it were not of key importance in understanding the King.

At the King's invitation, the actor Josef Kainz joined him in 1881 on a trip to Lake Lucerne in Switzerland, following in the footsteps of William Tell. Here, the young actor declaimed passages from the works of Friedrich Schiller to the King. Drawing by Hans Stubenrauch, c. 1920.

Ludwig himself made no attempt to hide the fact that women held little attraction for him. When the philosophy professor Johannes Huber, who held several confidential conversations with the King in 1864/1865, told Ludwig »*that the love of women could not fill a man's life, that it was more or less an episode in the life of the strong, manly nature*«, the King replied that in the case of some men this episode did not occur at all – he was referring to himself.

The Austrian ambassador Gustav Blome sent word to Vienna that the decorations from the ballet theatre but no female ballet dancers had made it into the King's bedroom

– this was apparently regarded as quite exceptional. *»So far he takes no pleasure in the company of ladies and in dealings with the female sex,«* he noted a year later. And Döllinger wrote to Charlotte Leyden in October 1865, updating her on the latest gossip: *»Our young master recently discovered that he had only a dim and confused idea of the ›nature of love‹; so he sent St*[ate] *C*[ouncillor] *Pfistermeister to – Wagner, with the instruction that he should get Wagner's opinion on love, its nature, its symptoms and so on, and then report this faithfully to him, the King.«* This shows Ludwig's insecurity and immaturity, but at this point the King was only twenty, after all, inexperienced both sexually and in matters of the heart.

The King developed close personal relationships only with men. He travelled with them, conversed with them for hours, went riding with them and invited them to his castles for long visits. Ludwig was also in contact with women, of course, including the actress Lila von Bulyowsky, who was invited to recite dramatic works to him and described him as *»cold as a fish!«* He was very fond not only of Sybilla von Leonrod, but also of Therese von Gasser, one of his mother's former ladies-in-waiting, and later of Czarina Maria Alexandrovna of Russia and finally of Elisabeth of Austria. But in all of these cases, and in a few others, his feelings were purely veneration of the respective woman's grace, mind, biography or artistic talent. He never sought physical closeness to women in the way he did to men – and this was not only owing to the social etiquette of the time. Rather, he found dealing with *»females« »annoying«*, as he admitted to Wagner in 1866.

DANGEROUS RUMOURS

»There is talk in Franconia and Swabia that His Majesty...is engaging in obscene acts with his two grooms [Joseph and Ludwig Völk], *that His Majesty is a spinach-cutter* [slang for someone engaging in anal intercourse] *and uses one of these Völk brothers for this...it casts a shady light on the King that he is so much and so exclusively in the company of his groom Völk; ...in*

Upper and Lower Franconia the rumour has spread that the King is engaging in illegal intercourse with men, yes, this rumour can be heard even in the royal stables,« Minister of Justice Eduard von Bomhard warned Cabinet Secretary Pfistermeister on 14 December 1865.

It cannot be ascertained whether Ludwig II actually carried out the rumoured sexual acts or whether his sexual activity remained restricted to masturbation and touching and kissing men, as he reports in his diaries.

It is certain, however, that the King shared the strict morals of his time, and that the step from *eros* to *sexus* – from sexual desire to actual sex – must have been an extremely difficult one for him. Moreover, Ludwig was highly religious and had been brought up to observe the sixth commandment (»Thou shalt not be unchaste!«). Even more important, however, was his understanding of himself as a King by Divine Right, appointed by the grace of God. Any sexual acts involving men would make him unworthy of this grace and endanger this fundamental pillar of his existence. In Ludwig's eyes, even masturbating and kissing made him a sinful being whose sins needed forgiveness through the holy sacrament of confession. He confessed his sins not only to his spiritual advisers, but also to his diary, in which he repeatedly invoked Jesus Christ, the Holy Virgin Mary, Saint Louis IX and the Bourbon monarchs to intercede for him.

The King wrote one of these diary entries in 1869 in the style of a decree: *»Au nom du Père, du Fils et du Saint Esprit! I lie in the sign of the Cross (Our Lord's day of redemption), in the sign of the sun (Nec pluribus impar!) and the moon (Orient! Rebirth through Oberon's horn of wonder. –) May I and my ideals be accursed if I should fall Thanks be to God it is no longer possible for I am protected by God's holy will, by the King's sublime word! – Mental love alone is permitted, sensual love by contrast is accursed. I solemnly pronounce an anathema* [that is, a church ban] *upon it…« »No more in January, no more in February, in general I must break myself of all of it as much as pos-*

sible,« he vowed, as well as *»My hands must not wander downwards a single time, under threat of severe punishment!«*

MANY CONTACTS

Over the course of his life, Ludwig had several longer-term friendships – with the theatre engineer Friedrich Brandt and the actor Emil Rhode, for example. He also had a large number of short, infatuated, informal friendships.

These contacts included the cavalry officer Lambert von Varicourt, Cabinet Secretary Friedrich von Ziegler and the Legation Secretary Anton von Hirschberg. His longest relationships included the aforementioned ones with his servants Karl Hesselschwerdt and Richard Hornig. He met both of them in 1866; their relationship was a close physical one which involved kisses and embraces. Furthermore, their signatures are to be found in Ludwig's diaries underneath entries formulated as vows:

> *»I most solemnly vow and declare…, over the course of the year that has just begun, as much as is possible to resist every temptation most bravely, not to give in to it if in any way possible, neither in word nor in deed, not even in thought. Thus to cleanse myself of all the impurities that sadly are part of human nature, and so to make myself more worthy of the Crown that God has bestowed upon me.«*
>
> *Diary entry Ludwig II, new year 1873*

The nature of the contacts Ludwig II had in his last years with many soldiers, mostly from the Third Chevauleger Regiment, who were his servants, cannot be defined. The fluctuation was considerable and Ludwig's harsh treatment of his staff notorious. Nevertheless, Ludwig also showed himself to be generous and loving towards them – adoring affection alternated with violence. There is no evidence of any sexual acts involving them, nor of sexual abuse.

Ludwig's persistent, futile attempts to suppress his inclinations not only sapped his strength but increased his despair. His ardent desire *»Beloved Karl, I long for your kiss...«* (1880s, to Karl Hesselschwerdt) was followed by attempts to purify himself. His constant remorse for his thoughts or deeds was accompanied by the resolution not to repeat them, even though Ludwig knew his struggle was in vain. He was not pure and sinless, like Lohengrin or Parsifal, as much as he strove to conform to this ideal.

»›Toute justice émane du Roy. – Si veut le Roy, veut la loi. – Une foi, une loi, un Roy.‹ – Louis« [»All law comes from the King – The King's will is law. – One faith, one law, one King. – Ludwig«]. This was the attitude, paired with his belief in purification through the Holy Grail, with which Ludwig hoped to win the battle against his own nature. He found his own leanings unacceptable, and this is reflected in his exaggerated and overblown concept of the ideal ruler.

»These buildings are my chief joy in life«

10 Castles as a symbol of divine right

»O, it is necessary to create such paradises, such poetic places of refuge, where for a brief time one can forget the dreadful world in which we live,« Ludwig wrote to Sybilla von Leonrod in January 1869, expressing a creed that he turned into reality through his planning and building of castles. Ludwig's »journeyman's pieces« in Hohenschwangau and Munich have already been mentioned. His living quarters in the Munich *Residenz*, which were splendidly furnished in the French baroque style, were the starting point for two palaces: Linderhof and Herrenchiemsee.

»In order to escape from wearisome life, from the restraints of the vexing, never-ending monotony of court ceremony that constrained him in the splendid chambers of the Temple of the King in Versailles, Louis XIV built the pleasure palace of Trianon. When this, too, grew and became palace-like, he erected the lonely, modest Marly, so he could breathe freely once more after the exertions of ceremonial life. – I would now also like to have a small pavilion built near…Linderhof…« With these lines of 28 November 1868, Ludwig II gave Councillor Lorenz von Düfflipp the order to construct a palace in the style of and in honour of the French king Louis XIV. Initially, his plans were modest. By September 1873, no less than seventeen different plans with layouts, front views and interior views had been produced to fulfil Ludwig's desire for his own castle in the mountains. Ludwig had known since childhood the secluded estate of Linderhof in the Graswang valley near Oberammergau, which was selected as the location where these dreams were to become reality. Maximilian II had now and again taken up residence here in the plain *»Königshäuschen«* (»the king's little house«) built in the style of a traditional

Alpine farmhouse; Ludwig took over this house when he became king and was equally fond of spending time there.

He gave his building project the name »Tmeicos Ettal«, an anagram of the Sun King's motto »L'état c'est moi« [»The state, it is I«], for Ludwig was modelling his plans more and more upon Versailles Palace. This royal seat was the centre of France's social and political life from the middle of the 17th century until 1789.

At the same time, the name »Tmeicos Ettal« was a reference to Ettal monastery, which was situated near Linderhof. Ettal had a central-plan church, and accordingly this code name also touched upon Ludwig's fascination with the Holy Grail: *»The Emperor Ludwig the Bavarian is supposed to have had the church in Ettal built according to the plans of the Grail temple; – the figure of Lohengrin rises before me once again,«* he wrote to Richard Wagner, telling him about the monastery church, which had been built by one of his 14th-century ancestors of the same name.

FRENCH SPLENDOUR IN THE BAVARIAN MOUNTAINS: LINDERHOF PALACE

Over the course of several years, Ludwig's plans for his palace went from a building with only one wing to a complex with five wings, a chapel and a theatre, seemingly a copy of its model Versailles. In any case, the projected palace was now far too large to be built in the narrow mountain valley near Linderhof.

As this problem started to become evident in the summer of 1870 and Ludwig wanted to experience at least a small piece of French splendour outside his Munich apartment, he gave orders for the *»Königshäuschen«* already standing in Linderhof to be extended. Over the years, this simple refuge was transformed into a large villa with a bedroom, dining room and study as well as four small corner rooms, all decorated in the Rococo style. Franz Seitz, set designer and Director of the Court Theatre, and the stage painter Christian Jank planned the palace's interior decoration, which drew

The dress carriage drawn by four white horses waits in front of Linderhof Palace's principal façade, ready for the King's excursion. – Photograph by Joseph Albert, c. 1884.

on models taken from Baroque and Rococo buildings; however, the copies had a distinctive touch all their own.

The demolition of the »*Königshäuschen*« made the complex fully consistent and homogenous; Georg von Dollmann was its architect. Tearing down the little house made it possible to add a further wing to round off the earlier extensions and to create a uniform exterior design based upon the style of Louis XIII and Louis XIV of France.

Work on the building, which is more reminiscent of a prestigious villa than a palace, dragged on into 1876, although the King used the first rooms as early as 1872. Construction would probably have lasted even longer had not 180 workers been employed for some stretches of time and a railroad been built to enable speedier transport of building materials.

The Chief Court Gardener Carl Joseph von Effner completed the plans for the gardens around the palace in 1874,

View of the garden front of Herrenchiemsee Palace with the north wing which remained unfinished at Ludwig II's death. It was demolished in 1907. – Coloured postcard, c. 1900.

and they were carried out by 1880. From that time on, Linderhof Palace has stood at the centre of a geometric park modelled on the French Baroque and the Italian Renaissance style, merging into an English landscape garden which is bordered almost seamlessly by the mountain forest.

»A TEMPLE OF GLORY«: HERRENCHIEMSEE PALACE

In 1873, the King bought the *Herreninsel* (»Monks' island«; the name refers to an old Augustinian monastery on the island) in Lake Chiemsee. The island provided him with a site large and secluded enough for the palace originally planned for Linderhof. Ludwig's aim here was to build a *»temple of glory«* for Louis XIV. Versailles Palace served as the direct inspiration for the façades and interiors, and its Hall of Mirrors and adjacent Peace and War Salons were copied almost exactly. The King's orders to his Court Secretary in December 1868 stated that the rooms *»must not be small, the mere illusion of size achieved by means of perspective is not enough to realise the majesty of that wonderful epoch...«*

Ludwig II studied the available sources intently, had dramas from the time of the Bourbons performed at the Munich Court Theatre with sets inspired by the rooms in Versailles and read all the related literature he could lay his hands on. The decoration of the interiors and the murals in Herrenchiemsee were to be based upon historical sources: »*There is a text on French coins, which feature the bust of Louis XIV in a true likeness; this work should be used as a model,*« stated the King; this is just one example of his attention to detail. During this time he sent his artists on several trips to Versailles and other palaces, including Augustusburg Palace in Brühl near Cologne, the *Residenz* in Würzburg and Fontainebleau near Paris. The artists then had to incorporate the things they had seen, particularly the interior decoration, into their plans, following the King's wishes.

Accordingly, Herrenchiemsee, the construction of which began in January 1878, is not just a copy of Versailles, but rather an enhancement of it – if not Ludwig's own creation. Based on descriptions, Ludwig had rooms built in Herrenchiemsee that actually no longer existed in Versailles (such as the »Escalier des Ambassadeurs«, a monumental flight of stairs). He also had rooms included in the building that had no counterpart in Versailles (such as the dining room).

The design of the façades and the gardens is also initially reminiscent of Versailles. Individual details were reproduced as exact copies of the original. But the choice of statues that adorn the palace's garden façade (they represent allegorically the dignity of kingship) and the fixtures in the two large fountains are not based on models from Versailles, but rather attest to Ludwig II's own artistic temperament and creative ideas for his palace, which went beyond simply copying an original.

The King had the idea of placing cone-shaped rocks with sculptures in the water basins directly in front of Herrenchiemsee after having seen photographs of the park of the royal palace La Granja de San Ildefonso near Madrid, which had similar fountains (this palace had been built in the 18th century by a grandson of Louis XIV).

In the north basin at Herrenchiemsee stands the fountain of the winged goddess of fame, Fama, with Envy, Deceit and Hate falling from the rock. In the southern basin we see Fortuna, the Roman goddess of fate and fortune, standing on a wheel on top of the rock.

***»Where I come to life again in delightful solitude, far away from the world that always denies me« –* Ludwig's true places of residence**

All over the world, Ludwig II is associated with his palaces Linderhof, Neuschwanstein and Herrenchiemsee. Many people assume that the King lived in these palaces. For the most part, visitors to his castles remain oblivious to the fact that Ludwig's real places of residence – the places that he visited most frequently and for the longest time, where he worked, dreamed, made politics and suffered – were actually elsewhere. And this is quite understandable, given that many of the King's places of residence were destroyed long ago, significantly altered or are inaccessible.

Both of Ludwig's chambers in the Munich *Residenz*, with its splendid conservatory, and Berg Castle on Lake Starnberg should feature among the most-visited sites associated with Ludwig; in both cases, however, only the outer shell (which has been altered) remains. Of the three domiciles used most frequently by Ludwig, only Hohenschwangau Castle has survived almost completely unchanged and is open to visitors.

By contrast, the King's many mountain cabins, *»where I revive in delightful solitude, far away from the world that always denies me«* (in a letter to Wagner, June 1867), are less suitable for great numbers of tourists. Some are situated between Lenggries and Füssen, others on the Pürschling and Brunnenkopf mountains near Linderhof and on the Hochkopf and Herzogsstand mountains by Lake Walchensee. For Ludwig, they were more than mere places to stay overnight when out hunting (they had been used for this purpose by his father Maximilian II and would be so again under Ludwig's successor Prince Regent Luitpold); they were important places of residence, in which the King enjoyed staying at least as much as in the palaces he had built for himself. Ludwig's many enthusiastic comments on the Alps *(»I yearn so for the mountains«)* were matched by his frequent and regular stays in these mountain cabins, some of which have survived to the present day.

The many coaching inns and other places of accommodation in Upper Bavaria and Tyrol at which the King stayed regularly are also worth mentioning at this point.

We can thus see that Ludwig II did not really inhabit the castles built for him. He knew them only as building sites (including Linderhof Palace, the only palace in which he lived for longer periods of time!). However, they remain the most visible expression of his ideas and his intentions to the present day.

SYMBOLIC PROGRAMME

Herrenchiemsee Palace is one of those castles which remained unfinished due to lack of funds and the King's early death. In order to understand it properly, we need to take account of its basic division into two groups of rooms. Ludwig II first entered the »Petits Appartements«, which represent a symbolic interpretation of the time of Louis XV of France. This is where Ludwig's private chambers were located, including his bedroom, decorated in shades of blue, and a study. Walking through a bare, unadorned, transitional passage, Ludwig II reached the »Grande Galerie«, the Mirror Gallery, from which he could gain access to all the other rooms in the »Grands Appartements«, all of which are designed as purely symbolic, monumental rooms. In the middle of palace – like in Versailles – is the »Chambre de Parade«, decorated completely in red. This state bedroom, which bears hardly any similarity to that in Versailles, was the first of the rooms to be completed in 1881 (Louis XIV saw his bed in Versailles as the centre of his kingdom and the world, claiming that the sun rose as he got up and sank as he went to bed).

This room at the centre of Herrenchiemsee stands for Ludwig's religious veneration of the Sun King: a textile image showing Louis XIV in his coronation robes is used on the back of the bed, which actually looks more like a throne. The Sun King is commended to the Virgin Mary by Saint Louis IX. This silk shading looks very like the main image on an altar. In this room, which is designed to be looked at and not used, a *prie dieu* – with an image of Saint Louis IX – stands right next to the monumental place of rest.

High above on the ceiling is a painting of »The Divine Morning«, with the god Apollo in the Chariot of the Sun. This god of purification and truth is also depicted in the ceiling fresco in the Stone Hall of Nymphenburg Palace, the room in which Ludwig II was christened and thus accepted into the fellowship of Christ in 1845. Ludwig decreed that the Nymphenburg fresco by Johann Baptist Zimmermann (1680–1758) be used as the model for the ceiling painting in the state bedroom in Herrenchiemsee. For the King, the fact that he was christened under the gaze of the god Apollo – the emblem of Louis XIV – was powerfully symbolic. It is thus hardly surprising that the Bavarian monarch emphasised his (in his eyes) »legitimate« connection to Louis XIV in the state bedroom of Herrenchiemsee.

A PALACE OF RIDDLES

The meaning of Ludwig II's largest and most expensive palace can also be detected in the »Salon de l'Œil de Boeuf« (Ox-eye Salon), which is modelled unmistakeably on Versailles. This is where the French crown princes were baptised. Ludwig not only had his version in Herrenchiemsee built on a larger scale, he also had an unusual ceiling fresco painted: Aurora (dressed in red) rises from the ocean in the East, while blue-clad Astraeus, the giant of the stars, goes to greet

Ludwig II had the »Cell of Gurnemanz« built in the Ammerwald Forest near Linderhof, modelled on the stage decorations for Wagner's »Parsifal«. This is where he retreated on Good Friday to pray. – Photochromic card, c. 1900.

her. This image does not draw upon any tradition and occurs neither in Versailles nor in any other picture before it. The painting – which features a star between the outstretched arms of Astraeus – is reminiscent of a detail in one of the baroque ceiling frescos in Ettal monastery.

In the christening chamber, the Sun King Louis XIV, who in Herrenchiemsee is associated with the colour red, encounters – in a figurative sense – the God of the Dusk. Astraeus stands for Ludwig II, King of Bavaria, a night-lover who favoured the colour blue. The symbolism deepens when we become aware that both rulers were born under the sign of Virgo and both their reigns began on the same day (10 March). For Ludwig II, these were no coincidences.

And so he was all the more keen for *»everything Bavarian ...to be removed in Chiemsee«*; this was his clear order to his artists and those in charge of building Herrenchiemsee. The palace was to contain no obvious visual reminders at all of the existence of a King of Bavaria.

LUDWIG'S WORLDS IN THE GRASWANG VALLEY

While Ludwig seldom visited the Herreninsel and his *»temple of glory«*, Linderhof Palace was one of his favourite residences. On the one hand, he preferred the area around Füssen and Oberammergau to the Chiemgau region (*»His Majesty is enamoured neither of this area nor of the lake and has no preference for them, it is art alone that must render the unpleasant pleasant and allow Him to forget the area and lake,«* the valet Lorenz Mayr wrote to Court Secretary Ludwig Bürkel in 1881), while on the other hand he had a number of other smaller buildings constructed in the Graswang valley, in keeping with his many interests.

Perhaps the most unusual of these is the artificial grotto with a lake named after Venus, the goddess of love, which was built by the landscape designer August Dirigl above the palace, using brick, cement and canvas. It imitates the blue grotto on Capri (Ludwig sent a servant to Capri twice to inspect the blue colour) and simultaneously refers to the opera »Tannhäuser«. According to legend, the eponymous hero spent some time in Venus' cave.

The lighting in the grotto (made possible by one of Bavaria's first electricity works) could be changed from red (Venus grotto) to blue (Capri), enhancing the fantasy world desired by the King.

The grotto was equipped with the latest technology, so that Ludwig II was able to enjoy both a waterfall and a wave machine. In addition to this, he had himself rowed about the lake in a shell-shaped boat (Lohengrin!) and bathed in the water, which could be heated.

The Linderhof park buildings were complemented by two oriental buildings (the Moroccan House and the Moorish Kiosk) and two cabins modelled on stage designs of Wagner operas. »Hunding's Hut« was built to imitate the set used in the première of Wagner's opera »The Valkyrie«. From 1876 on, this *»chamber of roughly hewn wood similar to the decoration of the first act«* evoked the world of Germanic legend. The stage directions for the third act of »Parsifal« served as the model for the Cell of Gurnemanz. From the summer of 1877 onwards, the King regularly withdrew here to pray, especially on Good Friday: »*There everything reminds me of that solemn morn of Good Friday in your blissful ›Parcifal‹, which pierced the depths of my soul with overwhelming force...On that holy ground I hear the portentous call of silver trumpets resounding from the Grail Castle; there I hear the holy chants of Montsalvat echoing down from the remote mountain; there I feel so happy, near that fountain where Parcifal was anointed, receiving the consecration of the true and authentic kingship that is achieved through humility and the destruction of all evil inside oneself,*« Ludwig told the composer in August 1877.

NEUSCHWANSTEIN, CASTLE OF THE GRAIL

The fantastic themes represented in many of the small buildings around Linderhof are also to be found the most famous castle that Ludwig had constructed. In Neuschwanstein near Füssen, the Nibelung legend meets Tannhäuser, Parsifal, Tristan and Isolde and Lohengrin – nor would the Orient, represented by a Moorish hall, have been left out, except that Ludwig II died before it could be built. Like Herrenchiemsee, Neuschwanstein is an unfinished palace that nevertheless reveals a great deal about its builder.

In 1867 Ludwig initiated a new production of Wagner's »Tannhäuser« in the National Theatre, and in May of that year travelled to the historical locations associated with this medieval minstrel, Wartburg Castle near Eisenach and the Hörselberg mountain, the location of Venus' cave, according to legend. On one of his trips to Paris two months later, Ludwig set eyes on Pierrefonds Castle, which was in the process of being restored as a private residence for Napoleon III.

»*I am currently reading some very interesting books about knighthood in the Middle Ages...for the last few days, I have been thinking of plans to rebuild the castle ruins near Hohenschwangau, which are very familiar and attractive due to their location; my aim is for the future castle to have more of the authentic, medieval character of an old knights' castle than the castle on Hohenschwangau,«* Ludwig announced to his cousin in Darmstadt on 25 April 1868. The monarch became more definite in a letter to Richard Wagner three weeks later: »... *the location is one of the most beautiful you could find, sacred and remote, a worthy temple for my divine friend, through whom alone the world gained salvation and true blessings. You will also find reminders of Thannhäuser (minstrel's hall with a view of the castle in the background), of Lohengrin (castle courtyard, open walkway, path to the chapel)...«* What at first sounded like a memorial to Wagner and his operas (the composer never saw this castle!) quickly became Ludwig II's own Grail Castle Montsalvat.

Work on the castle's construction began in February 1869. Four years later, Ludwig moved into his first living quarters in the gatehouse and watched the progress made on the other four parts of the building (palas, knights' house, bower and keep), which were constructed in Romanesque style. In the main building, the palas, the initially most important and highest room was an imitation of the ceremonial hall in the Wartburg, decorated with murals depicting the legend of Parsifal. Here – as in the castle as a whole – the King's guiding principle was that *»the pictures in the new castle should follow the legend and not the Wagnerian versions«*. An individual iconography was developed for each room by the King and the literary historian Hyazinth Holland.

Over the years, the throne room became the castle's central hall. It looks like a Byzantine church, and not just because of its gold colour. Even though a throne was supposed to stand in the place where one would expect to see an altar (Ludwig's death prevented the execution of this plan), the motifs of the wall paintings are clearly religious. They represent canonised kings – including Louis IX – as well as Jesus Christ, Mary, John the Baptist and the twelve apostles, the three wise men and Moses with the Tablets of the Law.

In his introduction to a new edition of the poem »Lohengrin«, the Catholic publisher and scholar Joseph Görres

(1776–1848) developed the hypothesis that the Byzantine church of Hagia Sophia in Constantinople had been the model for medieval descriptions of the Grail Temple. Ludwig was familiar with Görres' text and had the throne room in Neuschwanstein built in the style of the Hagia Sophia. As the Byzantine emperors took up the theme of divine right directly in their main church, two worlds of ideas came together for the Bavarian king: the idea of the divine right of kings and the idea of the power of the Holy Grail.

»STRENGTH GAINED FROM THE LILY«

The royal apartment on the third floor of the palas of the »New Castle Hohenschwangau« (as Ludwig II called his first large building project) was completed in the spring of 1884. The bedroom, which unlike the other rooms is decorated completely in the Gothic style, reveals Ludwig's thoughts.

In the bedroom, the murals and the sculptures refer to the story of Tristan and Isolde, a tale of forbidden and unfulfilled love.

The bed does not look like a place for even brief repose, but instead recalls a royal tomb with a canopy of gothic pinnacles. At the foot of the bed is a relief of Christ's resurrection. The rich textiles used throughout the room are embroidered not only with the Bavarian diamond coat of arms and with swans, but also with lilies. Ludwig noted in his diary: »*Strength gained from the lily to resist all temptations through the whole year,*« and »[absolved] *by the invigorating, strengthening scent of the Royal Lily.*« He wrote this sitting in his bedroom in a throne-like armchair, which looked directly at a small chapel opposite with the image of Louis IX on the altar (in the 12th century, the French king Louis VII included the lily, which like the swan is a symbol of chastity and purity, in the royal coat of arms as the stylised ornamental »fleur de lis«).

When the King died, a picture of Louis XIV was standing on the table in the living room of Neuschwanstein, which is decorated with images taken from the Lohengrin myth. The

Sun King was thus a guest in the room of the Guardian of the Grail. This shows once again that for Ludwig II, the Bourbons and Lohengrin were two closely related and not contradictory worlds.

***»There are serious impediments to my endeavour«* – The debt-ridden King**

Ludwig II's buildings, his passion for the theatre, his support of Richard Wagner and his habit of generously distributing gifts, cost a lot of money. The King covered all of these costs and more besides from his civil list. The civil list included the funds allocated to the constitutional monarch or, to be precise, the cabinet treasury. This treasury administered the King's finances. Ludwig had to use this to cover all of his expenses as ruler of Bavaria, including the pensions of former staff, the upkeep of the royal households and all of his castles and palaces, the Court Theatre and further positions. This also included maintaining his grandfather, the former King Ludwig I, whose household expenses made up around a quarter of the civil list until his death in 1868.

The introduction of the mark as currency throughout the Reich necessitated a new Finance Act in 1876, following which Ludwig received more than 4.2 million marks (one mark equalled roughly 6 euros) annually. Besides this, between 1879 and 1883 Ludwig also drew around 5 million marks from family capital reserves. In addition, he received the same amount in payments from Bismarck.

As high as this total sum seems, Ludwig's expenses were equally high. In 1877 at the latest it became clear that the cabinet treasury was in trouble. Ludwig's buildings were devouring more money than the King had at his disposal. This was one of the reasons for his Court Secretary's resignation. Richard Wagner also felt the consequences of this situation, as Ignaz von

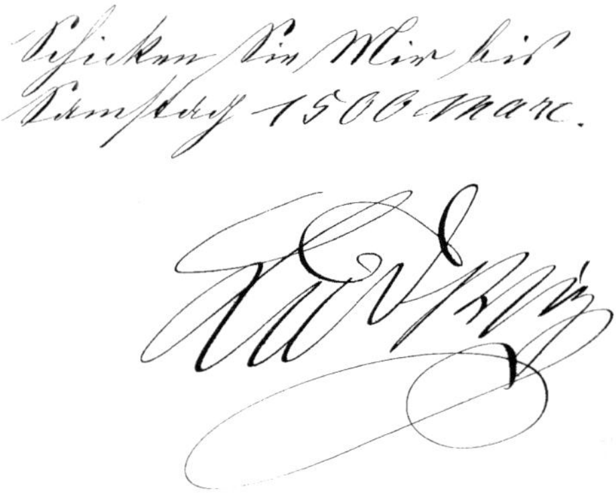
Schicken Sie Mir bis Samstag 1500 Mark.

Ludwig

The King required large sums of money for his many castles, the theatre and the conservatory on the roof of the Munich Residenz. For special purchases, Ludwig also occasionally needed large sums in cash, which he ordered in writing from the court treasury. These lines were written around 1880.

Döllinger wrote to Charlotte Leyden in August 1877: *»Richard Wagner was here to try and wrangle a significant sum of money out of the King...; however, he failed, as the civil list is vastly in debt.«*

The ministers had tried to keep out of the monarch's financial affairs, but by 1884 the mountain of debt had grown to 8.25 million marks and a constitutional crisis was looming. Unpaid bills of craftsmen and artists meant that legal action against the cabinet treasury and thus against the King seemed likely; the monarchy's reputation was at risk. *»If the present debts are not paid very soon, there is a risk that hundreds, perhaps even more livelihoods will fall into economic ruin, and this fact alone represents a grave danger, as the justified complaints of those affected...will resonate so widely that there will be no way of preventing them from reaching the steps of the throne,«* Minister of Finance Emil von Riedel appealed to Ludwig.

A loan from a banking consortium meant that the most urgent bills could be paid. Riedel remained concerned and advised the King strictly to avoid fresh debt in order to avert any threat to the throne and the state. But Ludwig, for whom building was the greatest joy in life, gave no thought to economising, only to continuing his building projects. *»It is My Royal Will that the buildings I have planned...be continued and completed. However, there are serious impediments to my endeavour due to the unfortunate state of my cabinet treasury. I entrust you, Sir Minister, with taking the necessary steps to regulate my finances and facilitate my undertakings...«*, Ludwig wrote, giving his Minister of Finance an order well-nigh impossible to carry out. At the same time, the King tried to get hold of money himself through persons he trusted. His request to withdraw four million marks from the private estate of his interned brother Otto failed due to the resistance put up by the prince's guardians. Adjutants and household officers were sent to royal courts and foreign governments to procure money. According to rumour, the King was thinking of robbing banks, but there is no evidence that this really was the case.

However, we do know what Ludwig took quite for granted in May 1886: that the Bavarian people were liable for his debts! He gave orders that it should be made clear to the people *»what heavy sacrifices, always felt by myself, I made in the German matter, which were all for the good of the people; that it is really a very small matter to request that the people cover all the debts of the* [cabinet] *treasury this one time.«* However, Johann von Lutz, the President of the Ministerial Council, refused to cover the deficits of the cabinet treasury using state funds. Minister of Finance Riedl supported him, pointing out that legally, the court and state budget were separate.

Nevertheless, there would have been basic political ways of supporting Ludwig's endeavours. Further-

Ludwig II on a night-time sleigh ride in the mountains of Schwangau. – Watercolour by Hans Stubenrauch, c. 1920.

more, Ludwig was not informed about all available debt relief options. For example, the information that various banks would have been happy to give him a loan never reached him. The plans of his ministers and parts of his family to depose the King, which his debts among other factors served to justify, were not to be endangered under any circumstances.

MEANING OF LIFE

Difficult though it is to deduce the individual references in Ludwig's castles, they prove that the building and decoration of his palaces was informed by a sophisticated, interconnected and highly individual concept. Unlike other aristocratic architecture of the same time, they were not conceived as demonstrations of power and a legitimation of the ruler who built them, but were rather an inward reflection of their builder, who withdrew from real life more and more. Ludwig was unable to realise kingship by divine right in the real world and thus created symbolic spaces in which he could experience it. These spaces – just like building in itself – provided him with support and gave his life meaning. Accordingly, they can be seen as the result of his insecurity.

When his personal and financial situation began to appear increasingly desperate in May 1886, he appealed to a confidant for help: *»These buildings are my chief joy in life. Since everything has come to such a shameful halt, I am constantly thinking of abdication, suicide. This condition must end, the building must falter no longer…My life's happiness depends upon it.«*

»I want to escape this damned, hellish gloom«

11 Ludwig's withdrawal from public life and his decline

On 16 July 1871, the Bavarian troops who had gone to war against France nearly one year earlier returned to Munich, where they were greeted enthusiastically by the population. The campaign had been victorious and the German Empire founded. The Prussian – and now German – Crown Prince Friedrich Wilhelm, who had assumed command of the Bavarian troops in 1870, rode through the cheering crowds at the head of the army. In the Odeonsplatz, Ludwig II, seated on horseback, took the salute of the military parade and greeted his Prussian relative. He referred to this moment as his *»first public appearance as a vassal«*.

The celebrations kept the entire city in a state of excitement. They included a military banquet for 1000 guests, held the following day, which Ludwig II, as head of state and Supreme Commander of the army, was expected to attend. The King failed to turn up, however – much to the annoyance of the other guests. The continuing victory and unification celebrations were too painful for Ludwig. The King preferred to receive his *»adored friend«* Richard Hornig in the conservatory of the *Residenz* *»after a long time of separation«* rather than give a toast to the Bavarian troops, their leader and the Crown Prince.

THE KING IN DENIAL

1871 marked a key turning point in Ludwig II's life. From then on, he reduced his public appearances (which had been seldom enough) to a bare minimum and only rarely gave audiences on official matters. He also refused to meet with other monarchs – with the exception of meetings with Kaiser Wilhelm in 1871 and 1874 – which often led to diplomatic difficulties. Ludwig II deplored the political situation and found the curtailing of his sovereignty unbearable: »*I want to escape this damned, hellish gloom, which is constantly trying to suck me into its miasma...far away from the profane, everyday world, from unholy politics, which tries to wrap me in its tentacles, hoping to suffocate all poetry entirely,*« he wrote to Wagner. He confessed to Sybilla von Leonrod: »*...for me, the political situation is simply too lamentable and alienates me more and more, and the prospects for the future seem devoid of comfort; especially since the last war, which ended in such glory for Bavaria in other regards, contributed to forcing me and the country into the iron grip of the damned Prussian-flavoured German Empire, this unholy war, which so many love so enthusiastically! This in particular is a curious but deeply deplorable twist of fate!*«

Ludwig now avoided personal contact with his ministers as much as possible, much like his father and grandfather, neither of whom had placed great value on direct contact with ministers. However, this attitude deprived him of the ability to influence political events in his own interests.

Ludwig could not have expressed his disappointment with the consequences of the founding of the Reich more clearly. While there is no political justification for this attitude of denial, it is understandable from a personal point of view. After all, Ludwig's long-held dream of a more strongly monarchic form of government had been shattered.

It was a collision of irreconcilable worlds: the King's vision of an absolute monarchy by divine right, and the popular demand for a constitutional monarch who showed himself to his people. Franz von Pocci (1807–1876), who for many years was Chief Treasurer to the Bavarian kings and wrote several children's stories about Kasperl (the German equivalent of Punch), wrote a critical poem at this time which was published only after his death: »*If you want to be a King ›by the grace of God‹...then show yourself worthy of God's grace. You remained a child upon the throne. The sceptre became a toy to you, a magic wand for idle fantasies, royal power seems to have given you only the ability to create fantastic fairy-tale images.«*

THE INCOMPATIBILITY OF DREAMS AND REALITY

The newspaper »Bayerisches Vaterland« asked in December 1871: »*Who is ruling Bavaria at present? Is Bavaria still a constitutional state in which the King takes decisions independently, without even consulting his ministers, or has constitutionalism actually progressed to the point that the state government... is the real regent?*« This question, published in the extreme Patriots' main paper, was not far removed from reality, but it laid its finger upon a contradiction: for Ludwig II, it was inconceivable that the state should be governed by ministers. It was his own withdrawal in reaction to the incompatibility of his dreams and reality that made this development possible in the first place, however. Bit by bit, his denial of the true situation gave the ministers more power and more responsibility for governance, weakening the monarchic principle. Of course, the ministers and officials were happy for the monarch to give them free rein for the most part and only seldom interfere in matters of governance.

THE POLITICAL KING

This does not mean that the King neglected the duties of his office or was uninterested in political events. Up to 1886, the year of his death, Ludwig was presented with and dealt with around a dozen petitions every day. Regardless of where the King was staying, Ludwig's decisions often landed back on the ministers' tables the following day. In the case of planned longer absences, such as his trips to France and Switzerland, Ludwig instructed his ministers to send him the files on which he needed to work in good time. He attached great importance to the smooth handling of official business. Even as late as 1883 the ministers were satisfied, and »*despite written correspondence, the royal signatures are received in good time,*« as the Austrian ambassador noted. Now and again

Ludwig would add a comment or question to these documents, but he rarely ordered the ministers' originals to be changed. The monarch lacked the strength and the will to pursue his decisions further. While Ludwig requested that he be informed of the Cabinet Secretary's or respective minister's further steps in matters important to him, any refusal on their part had no consequences – apart from awakening the King's displeasure.

In his rare audiences and discussions on political issues, the King was always well informed and took a clear stance. In 1873, for example, Felix Dahn, the author of the novel »Ein Kampf um Rom« (»A Struggle for Rome«), was granted an audience that lasted almost six hours: it was *»fortunate that I had studied the German Imperial Constitution...so closely. For the King, whose detailed knowledge of these matters was astonishing, asked probing questions, often concerning the smallest individual details of the Treaties of Versailles! He showed himself to be as well informed as he was intelligent; his responses were sharp, even somewhat nit-picking, dialectic and subtle.« »King Sun II«*, as Dahn called Ludwig in his notes, was also interested in the population's opinion of him.

Even at a distance, Ludwig was always attentive and demanded a minimum level of deference to his royal status. For example, he stipulated that his Cabinet Secretaries – the only state officials he still permitted to speak to him in person – should submit matters not only orally but also in writing, so that he could give them his thorough attention. In 1872 Ludwig II reiterated his order that all important letters and documents sent to foreign governments be presented to him for inspection.

CONTRADICTIONS

On two occasions, Ludwig did actually take a more active part in domestic politics than the ministers would have liked. In June 1872, after the death of the incumbent President of the Ministerial Council, the King requested Rudolf von Grasser, who was close to him, to form a new and expressly anti-Reich ministry. However, following protest by nearly all important political figures and a change in his own opinion, Ludwig abandoned this plan that ultimately would have resulted in a change of the system. Someone other than Grasser was appointed Minister for Foreign Affairs and President of the Ministerial Council.

Similarly, after the *Landtag* elections of 1875, the King initially attempted to implement policies focused upon Bavarian interests with a new prime minister. This would have accommodated the Patriots, who again held a majority in the *Landtag* (even though the King had permitted the electoral boundaries to be redrawn in the Liberals' favour). In the end, however, he was of the opinion – as he had been in 1872 – that taking account of the electoral will would strengthen parliamentarianism to the monarchy's detriment. He failed to recognise that this only increased the distance between himself and his people, while simultaneously confirming the power of the liberal ministers.

»*The Social Democrat threat*« – Ludwig's fear of revolution and assassination

From 1868 onwards, it could no longer be ignored that the number of those joining workers' organisations was growing steadily. Ludwig reacted with great concern and studied the reports of the Ministry for the Interior on social-democratic activity attentively. Although this could not be termed a mass movement, the King feared that public order was under threat – and he also feared for his own safety.

»*The King wishes...for a report..., on the reasons that the Social Democrats have grown in number in Nuremberg in particular, what favourable living conditions Nuremberg in particular offers to these ideas, and then whether it is not time...for something to be done against the mischief of social-democratic agitation,*« his Cabinet Secretary wrote to a friend in January 1877. During the 1870s in Bavaria, the Social Democrat movement was concentrated in Nuremberg, Augsburg and a few other smaller towns – regions in which industrialisation, the precondition for the formation of a working class, had advanced further than in other parts of this agrarian state.

Even though all social classes coexisted comparatively peacefully in his kingdom, Ludwig gave orders for the authorities to crack down upon the Social Democrats early on. In 1873 he suggested a more consistent application of the Law on Associations to make it more difficult for people to assemble. However, in the first years the officials' reaction was either non-existent or placatory.

Ludwig grew increasingly displeased with this passive behaviour, which changed only after the leftist party gained a massive increase in votes in the 1878 *Reichstag* elections (rising to 500,000, up from 124,000 in 1871). The King's personal fear of Social Democrats and anarchists – which for him were one and the same – increased still further after two assassination attempts were made upon Kaiser Wilhelm I that same year. Despite the fact that no links to any political party could be proven, Imperial Chancellor Bismarck proposed the »Law against the public danger of Social Democratic endeavours«, which was also supported by Ludwig II, who spoke to Bismarck of the *»social-democrat threat«*. After this voicing of royal support, the Bavarian government agreed to the regulations set out in the »Socialist Act«, which were in force from 1878 to 1890.

After the assassination of Czar Alexander II of Russia on 1 March 1881, Ludwig's fear of socialism escalated to a panic-stricken terror of conspiracy – aside from the political dimension, his distress now had a definite psychological dimension as well. The King insisted on tighter security measures for his drives and walks in the *Englischer Garten* in Munich, which had in any case become infrequent. When he left the train in Laim near Munich and drove to the *Residenz* in a carriage, mounted guards now lined his route. In Munich, he was surrounded by large numbers of police. The extent to which Ludwig was consumed by this fear of assassination can be seen from a contemporary story: he fled from a church after a policeman had dropped his helmet and the King thought the crack with which it hit the ground was a gunshot. It is striking that he feared for his life most in the city – that is, in Munich. By contrast, for the most part he felt safe in the Bavarian uplands. This is certainly one of the reasons that Ludwig withdrew from public and ceremonial life in the Bavarian capital. Withdrawal was encouraged further by an actual threat aimed directly at Ludwig. Following his consent to the »Socialist Act«, he had received threatening letters. In February 1884, an anonymous author in the Zurich magazine »Der Sozialdemokrat« (»The Social Democrat«) even called for the King of Bavaria, whose *»character is corrupted,«* to be declared legally incapable.

What did Ludwig do to stop the growing politicization of the working classes and the threat this posed in his eyes? While Bismarck hoped that progressive social laws would destroy the basis for the Social Democrats' success, Ludwig had no plan at all. Even as late as the 1860s he had paid little heed to social legislation in his own country, although he was always interested in the individual fortunes of his subjects and spent significant amounts on social causes. Rather, Ludwig II thought the only way to deal effectively with issues was to stress his authority as monarch. The following statement by Ludwig (undated, but vouched for by the cavalry captain Paul von Haufingen) shows how out of touch he was: *»I consider the fitting solution to the social question in my country to be* *of greater importance than if I could become lord over Europe through famed military exploits, and I do not wish to be responsible for the loss of even one of my citizens' lives for selfish purposes. I wish for my Creator…to grant me the good fortune that people will say after my death: Ludwig strove only to be the truest, best friend to his people and he succeeded in making his people happy.«* The will was there – but he lacked the appropriate means.

One reason for Ludwig's continued dislike of the Patriots was the doctrine of papal infallibility pronounced in July 1870 in St Peter's Basilica in Rome. Ludwig feared that the Catholic clergy who dominated the Patriots' Party would seek to curtail his traditional royal privileges. He saw the Curia's decision as a deliberate expansion of clerical power to include secular matters. This was the reason he supported the so-called *»Kulturkampf«* (»culture struggle«) that Bismarck initiated against the Catholic clergy and had it implemented and administrated by his own Minister of Culture Johannes Lutz, who was likewise convinced that the doctrine of infallibility represented a threat to the state's political and social order. The tense situation in the Reich only calmed down in 1878.

Ludwig was very religious, had *prie-dieux* in all his palaces and always had a portable altar set up in even the most remote cabins. However, as early as 1865 the Munich professor Johannes Huber had been surprised by his free-thinking religious beliefs and disparaging remarks about the clergy. The King made a strict distinction between faith and the Church. Thus his reaction to his mother Marie's conversion to the Catholic faith in 1874, at the height of the conflict with political Catholicism in Germany, was ambivalent.

Incidentally, Ludwig was always present when new bishops took their oath on the Bavarian Constitution, despite his dislike of public appearances, as he wanted to emphasise his royal position to the clergy.

LONELINESS, A HEAVY BURDEN

»In dear, poetry-laden Hohenschwangau, in the beloved mountains, by the shores of the magnificent lake, on the mountaintops, in the lonely cabin or the Rococo splendour of my chambers in Linderhof it is my greatest delight, which never ceases, to immerse myself in the study of captivating works (mainly historical in content) and there to find solace and balm for much that is bitter and painful, entailed by the sad present, the 19th century that is so abhorrent to me,« Ludwig II wrote to Sybilla von Leonrod in 1874, telling her of his pain and his true interests. This was the last year that he took part in the Corpus Christi procession, one of the Bavarian ruler's most important ceremonial duties, and attended the opening of the *Oktoberfest*. The following year saw his last public appearance, during a military parade, as Supreme Commander of the Bavarian army.

Ludwig's appearance had also changed greatly, not least because he was becoming increasingly nocturnal. His face had become pale and his body corpulent, the suits he wore were increasingly ill-fitting and he was less and less the image of the radiant youth he had been in his early years as king – and probably even less like the royal figure he longed to be himself.

When the House of Wittelsbach's 700th anniversary as rulers of Bavaria came round in 1880, the King could bring himself only to make a written statement to his people, in which he declared that *»the happiness of my faithful people is the aim of my most ardent desires, it is the condition of my own happiness.«* Ludwig shied away from the public appearance recommended by his court secretary: *»I can no longer bear to be stared at by thousands of people, to smile and wave a thousand times, direct questions at people I have nothing to do with and hear answers that I am not interested in. No! No! I can no longer give up my solitude!«* However, this self-imposed loneliness became a torture to him as well: *»If my life did not run like clockwork, I would be unable to bear my solitude, and it is often a heavy burden.«*

SOLITARY IMMERSION IN OTHER WORLDS

Ludwig hated Munich and in recent years had spent scarcely more than the twenty-one days specified in the Constitution there. During his time in the capital, privately held theatrical and operatic performances enabled him to immerse himself in other worlds. Between May 1872 and May 1885, 209 of these private performances were given in the theatre of the *Residenz* and the Court and National Theatre. Most of these were plays (154), and Ludwig took charge of their selection, cast and décor. The majority of the pieces staged were set in 17th- or 18th-century France and represented the Bourbon kings in their greatest splendour and majesty. The King also commissioned court poets to write plays about historical events of his choosing. He was keen to experience history on the stage in a form as close to reality as possible. As if on a journey back in time, he demanded the greatest possible accuracy both in the costumes and in the events portrayed; engravings and contemporary reports were used as authentic sources. »*Please inform the poet that the declaration of the Duke of Anjou of Spain did not take place in the bedroom, but in a so-called Grand Cabinet. Order an engraving by Gérard from Paris that represents this scene, in the last act the actors should take the same positions as on the image,*« ran one of the royal instructions to the court secretary responsible.

The stage designs also corresponded with Ludwig's building plans. On the Munich stage, he was able to try out and experiment with space and form before solidifying them in the stone architecture of his castles. It was no coincidence that theatre painters and stage designers were involved in planning the castles and producing designs.

Ludwig's justification for these elaborate special performances meant for his eyes only, some of which were later taken into the theatres' official programme, was that »*Theatre cannot be an illusion for me as long as I am constantly stared at by the people, my every facial expression followed through their opera glasses. I want to watch, not be an object watched by the masses.*«

»Otherwise it will be a castle in the air« – Ludwig's last castle

The plan should remain secret, the King's confidant counselled: *»As to the Falkenstein, the most wonderful spot in the Allgäu, the purchase of this land would require secret negotiations.«* Ludwig II read Richard Hornig's advice on 9 May 1884. A year earlier, the Bavarian monarch had voiced a wish to build a castle on the site of the highest ruins in Bavaria, Falkenstein Castle near Pfronten in the Allgäu, which was only around twenty kilometres from Neuschwanstein as the crow flies.

Because of Ludwig II's immense debts, it was necessary to keep this new building project secret. Instead of following his ministers' advice and curbing his building activities, Ludwig bought the ruins of Falkenstein Castle through a front man.

Without waiting for the Munich banks to grant him a loan, Ludwig II commissioned Georg von Dollmann to draw up first plans for a »robber baron's castle« in early 1884. These sketches looked very different from a first imaginative depiction of the castle that theatre painter Christian Jank had produced without taking into account the lack of space on the mountain top. Although the monarch was aware that Jank's picture was only an unfeasible view of a future castle, he decided Dollmann's austere model was too small and ignoble. He relieved the architect, who had worked for him since 1868, of all his duties. At this point Richard Hornig became involved once again. At the King's command, he hired Max Schultze, the *Oberbaurat* (head surveyor) of the Princes of Thurn and Taxis in Regensburg, as chief architect for Falkenstein – bypassing all the court authorities in Munich who should have been responsible. Schultze, who at that time was busy rebuilding the south wing of St Emmeram Palace, was happy to accept this private commission and presented his first plans for the construction of the castle in September 1884.

Schultze's work was monitored ceaselessly by the impatient monarch, who dispatched Richard Hornig to Regensburg. Ludwig instructed his emissary not to forget Falkenstein among all his other projects and building work, »*otherwise it will be a castle in the air.*« At the same time he stressed: »*Falkenstein must not be built at the expense of the Chiemsee Palace* [Herrenchiemsee Palace] *and the new castle in Hohenschwangau* [Neuschwanstein Castle].« It became increasingly difficult for Richard Hornig to manage the balancing act between the »dos« and the »don'ts« demanded by the King.

In the meantime, Max Schultze was also being driven to distraction by Ludwig, who rejected the architect's plan to design Falkenstein Castle in a uniform Gothic style. Instead, the monarch commanded that a large bedroom in the Byzantine style be built at the centre of the complex. The architect objected that there was not enough space on the mountain top for the desired chamber with its high cupola.

The shell of Falkenstein was supposed to be complete by the end of 1885. By this time, a road to the mountain-top and a water supply line had already been built through the efforts of sixty-four labourers. However, all other work on the architect's part was delayed by the King's many requests for changes. Ludwig was focusing increasingly on the design of the bedroom, which was developing into a church-like sacred space, a continuation of the style and the ideas of the throne room in Neuschwanstein.

Neuschwanstein Castle as a building site, without the knights' house and the bower. The King was able to move into his chambers on the third floor of the palas, which can be seen here, in 1884. – Photograph, 1880. ▶

More and more plans were sent to the King from Regensburg, including a *»complete model of the castle most humbly presented for inspection«* (Hornig to Ludwig II), which ended up on the third floor of Neuschwanstein Castle. Schultze never met the King in person; all contact was through the Court Secretariat or the equerry. However, the Regensburg architect did travel to Pfronten himself in order to gain an impression of the building site.
In September 1885 Schultze handed back his contract; he believed there was no chance that his plans would ever be realised. Ludwig II subsequently commissioned the architect Julius Hofmann, who was also in charge of the building of the King's other castles, to continue the Falkenstein project. Hofmann attempted to accommodate the larger dimensions demanded by the King in his plans, suggesting the removal of more rock and increasing the area of the castle's foundations through brickwork.
One of the members of staff was sketching a new version of the bedroom when the news of the King's death arrived. Not only this sketch of the room remained unfinished; Ludwig II's dream castle on the peak of the Falkenstein mountain, close to the clouds, was also never completed. Throughout the entire planning process for Falkenstein, the bedroom was the room most important to Ludwig. The King specified an ever larger and higher hall, the sacred appearance of which was modelled on Byzantine architecture. The mosaic floor corresponds to that of the bedroom in the Imperial Palace in Constantinople, with the peacock, a symbol of resurrection, at its centre. However, the architectural similarity to the throne room in Neuschwanstein is even more striking. Instead of a throne, the apse would have contained a bed, and on a mural above the bed the Holy Virgin and the Christ Child would have kept watch

over the sleeping King. The bed, more like a throne or a baldachin than a place of rest, was to be framed by two candelabras (like an altarpiece and similar to the arrangement in the conference chamber in Herrenchiemsee Palace). A sculptured dove was to hang from the ceiling on a long cord directly above the steps up to the bed – like the image of the Holy Ghost in a church. The washstand in the bedroom in Falkenstein was conceived as a combination of font and tabernacle. In the transitions between the square central area and the cupola, angels seated upon clouds were to bear the symbols of kingship (crown, sword, orb and sceptre). Above this, a painted frieze of the apostles and a blue, starry ceiling would have represented the heavenly and divine sphere.
Why was Ludwig, who always thought in signs, symbols and allegories and planned his castles accordingly, so concerned with the bedroom in Falkenstein? Was it to be a last chance to cleanse himself of his sins, or an apotheosis of his understanding of kingship? The shape and the position of the bed give us one possible answer: in art-historical tradition, the room suggests a mausoleum, the burial place of a Christian ruler with the hope of resurrection.

»IT IS A QUAGMIRE«

From 1885 onwards, Ludwig's withdrawal from society, the costs associated with his castles and private theatrical performances, and his behaviour in general were discussed in the press, especially the press outside Bavaria. The »Frankfurter Zeitung« in particular was extremely critical, while more government-friendly papers in Munich still referred to *»the King's private affairs«*. In July 1885, the Frankfurt newspaper declared: *»These conditions are not conducive to strengthening the monarchy.«* One month later, they again wrote: *»It is not good for a monarch to cut himself off from his people, arranging his life so that he needs to interact only with* *those immediately surrounding him…The idea of republicanism is foreign to the majority of Bavarian people, but here and there the idea is voiced that a king is not absolutely necessary for a state to exist.«*

The ministers, led by the President of the Ministerial Council, Johannes Lutz (in office since 1880), had also become concerned for the monarchy's reputation by now, even though for years they had refrained from acting as they benefited from the situation. However, reports of the King's tantrums, the orders and commissions he bombarded his staff with (mainly concerning his buildings) and the fact that most of his dealings were with low-ranking people (Ludwig received his Cabinet Secretary for the last time in 1885) called for a reaction. As early as 1882, Friedrich von Ziegler, who was Cabinet Secretary at the time, had written to a colleague: *»It is a quagmire that we are in. If you want to take action, I will too – but in any case, the catastrophe will not be long in coming. Everyone is fed up. The manner in which people are treated is simply unbelievable!«*

> *»Most Serene and mighty King! Most merciful King and Lord! As one of the favoured ones who have the high privilege and the good fortune to lay best wishes for the New Year at Your Royal Majesty's feet in writing, I approach the King I love so ardently. My heart, which is Your Majesty's entirely, asks of kind Providence to bestow that which is still lacking for Your Royal Majesty's perfect happiness. May your every wish, your every will be granted immediately, may vexation and worry never blight Your Majesty's days, and may blooming health be Your Majesty's companion for a long, long time to come…«*
>
> *Richard Hornig, the King's confidant, on 31 December 1884 to Ludwig II*

SWAN SONG FOR A KING

In the spring of 1886, the catastrophe was indeed imminent. Ludwig was reluctant to reduce his mountain of debt by economising in the castle-building, and so he considered asking the *Landtag* for help. The Patriots held the majority in the *Landtag*, however. While they agreed with the Liberals that involving the *Landtag* was not an appropriate way of reducing the King's debt, they remained an element of uncertainty for the government. It could not be ruled out that the Patriots might after all offer the King their support in return for political concessions – which would be disadvantageous to the governing Liberal ministers and their officials.

For Lutz and his colleagues, there was only one way out of this situation. While it was not possible simply to depose Ludwig, the Bavarian Constitution contained a certain passage, according to which it was possible to install a regent, should the ruling monarch foreseeably be prevented from exercising his office for over a year.

Accordingly, they needed to find such an impediment and convince the person next in line to the throne of their plan.

Otto's illness meant that Ludwig's brother was not an option, and so Prince Luitpold, the third son of Ludwig I, was the potential successor. However, Ludwig's uncle's reaction to the suggestion that he might take over the regency was at first non-committal.

Towards the end of March 1886, Johann von Lutz summoned Bernhard von Gudden, a renowned professor of psychiatry. Following a meeting of forty-five minutes, in which Lutz explained the King's strange behaviour and the current situation, the doctor offered to provide a medical evaluation that would confirm the King's *»constitutional madness«*.

Over the following weeks, the former Cabinet Secretaries Friedrich von Ziegler and Ludwig von Müller, the Ministerial Secretary Friedrich von Thelemann, Equerry Richard Hornig, the Quartermaster of the Royal Stables Karl Hesselschwerdt and the servants Adalbert Wecker and Lorenz Mayr all reported strange facts about the King and his life to Gudden – they were testifying against him.

At the end of this process, an evaluation was produced by the doctors Gudden, Friedrich Wilhelm Hagen, Hubert

Grashey and Max Hubrich which completely convinced the hesitant Luitpold. He agreed to the legal incapacitation of his nephew Ludwig II in a meeting with Lutz and other ministers, and on 9 June took over the regency.

These plans did not remain secret, as may be seen in press reports, including by the Viennese newspaper »Neue Freie Presse«, which wrote as early as the beginning of May 1886 *»that the King is gravely ill and the appointment of a regent may only be a matter of weeks,«* and the Augsburg »Postzeitung«, which reported on 2 June that *»there are no thoughts of a ›coup d'état‹; if necessary, everything will be carried out according to the Constitution.«*

The only one to remain oblivious was Ludwig himself. He had been staying in Neuschwanstein Castle since 2 June, without any apparent changes to his daily routine.

12 The end and the beginning

On 11 July 1886, it poured with rain. When night fell, the King was alone in Neuschwanstein Castle, which was still under construction. Ludwig's last hours in the medieval dream-world he had built in stone had begun.

A servant noticed the Bavarian King wandering around his castle. Ludwig lingered for a particularly long time in the throne room, which even incomplete still outshone all other rooms in its size and splendour. Six canonised kings, the representatives of the highest kingly perfection for Ludwig, looked down on him from the apse. Could the music of Wagner's »Parsifal« have been in his ears, music that – in his understanding – reminded him of the sanctity of the king appointed by God? His farewell to the throne room was to be a farewell for ever.

In Neuschwanstein, the Bavarian King experienced the greatest conceivable downfall.

Only seven weeks previously, on Good Friday, Ludwig had ascended Mount Calvary near Füssen on his own and had been seen there deep in prayer: *»Before the monarch turned away from the station* [of the Cross], *he lifted his face to the cloudy skies. His desperate gaze, full of sadness and pain, long remained focused on the heavens, where he seemed to be searching for God. Then he brushed his right hand over his face to hide his tears,«* the vicar of St Mang in Füssen reported. On 6 June, the King attended the Sunday church service in the chapel of Hohenschwangau Castle, as was his wont.

THE CAPTURE OF THE KING

In the early hours of 10 June, posters informed the population of Munich that Prince Luitpold had taken over the regency of Bavaria. At the same time, the committee that was supposed to take Ludwig to Berg Castle was arrested and

The throne room in Neuschwanstein in the year of Ludwig's death. While the large chandelier that visitors can see today was commissioned by Ludwig, it was only completed and hung in the room in 1904. – Photograph, 1886.

subsequently released in Hohenschwangau. They had proceeded completely amateurishly.

In the night between 11 and 12 June, God forsook the King: a second committee led by Bernhard von Gudden arrested him in Neuschwanstein. Von Gudden informed the utterly bewildered Ludwig that four psychiatrists had declared him insane: »*Your Majesty is mentally disturbed to a very advanced degree, in fact You are suffering from that form of mental illness that experienced psychiatrists familiarly refer to as paranoia – (madness).*« The doctor told Ludwig that he would be taken to Berg Castle for his own safety that same night.

»*Oh! What do you want? What is all this about?*«, the King replied, continuing: »*How can you declare me mad, you have not looked at or examined me?«* Gudden pointed to the overwhelming amount of documentary evidence, which had rendered any personal examination unnecessary.

Now Ludwig, who despite forewarnings had refused to follow the advice of those closest to him and flee to Austria, was in the hands of the second committee consisting of two doctors, five wardens, one police captain and an equerry. At twelve past noon on 12 June, they arrived in Berg on Lake Starnberg. Changes had been made to the castle since Ludwig's last visit one month earlier: spyholes had been added to the doors to the King's private chambers, the door handles on the inside had been removed, and the windows had been barred. Now Ludwig was held captive in one of his favourite castles.

On the evening of 13 June, von Gudden and Ludwig set out on a walk around the castle grounds. The doctor gave express orders that they should not be accompanied by a guard. On their first walk together that afternoon, they had been accompanied by two male nurses.

By eight in the evening, the two had not returned, even though there had been heavy rain showers, and a search operation was started.

UNEXPLAINED DEATH

According to official reports, the lifeless bodies of King Ludwig and Bernhard von Gudden were discovered floating in the lake at eleven at night. Around midnight, following several attempts at resuscitation, they were declared deceased.

The official statement said that the King had drowned after forcing Gudden underwater. The »Bundeszeitung niederbayerischer Landwirte« wrote in 1894 that if everyone who doubted the royal catastrophe were arrested, *»then soon the prisons would not be sufficient to hold them.«* To this day, the exact circumstances of the deaths of Ludwig II of Bavaria and his appointed doctor have not been resolved. Accordingly, on 13 June 1886 a myth was born that to this day allows people to identify themselves with Bavaria through the

While Ludwig's body rests in the royal crypt in St Michael's Church in Munich, his spirit lives on. The Viennese newspaper »Der Floh« published this representation of his apotheosis on 20 June 1886 under the title »The Swan King«. In the background on the right-hand side, we can see Berg Castle, the King's last place of residence, with its distinctive tower »Isolde«.

person of this king. Ludwig II has also become the royal cult symbol *par excellence*. During his own lifetime, however, this veneration was denied him.

»He was a king – and he died of it!«, wrote Fritz Ostini, one of the founders of the art and literature journal »Jugend«, in 1902. One need hardly say more.

> *»...one [cannot] but think how all might have been different if beloved Ludwig's manner had been treated more sparingly, more understandingly! As it is, one's heart bleeds at the thought of how he was first taken from us with such lies and deception and then driven to extremity in such an outrageous manner.«*
>
> *Prince Wilhelm of Hesse to his aunt, Queen Mother Marie of Bavaria, Darmstadt, 13 June 1887.*

Chronological table

1811 28 November: Maximilian (later Maximilian II. Joseph, King of Bavaria), the father of Ludwig II, is born in Munich as the eldest son of Crown Prince Ludwig (from 1825 King Ludwig I) and his wife Therese von Sachsen-Hildburghausen.

1821 12 March: Prince Luitpold, the later Prince Regent (1886–1912), is born as the third son of Crown Prince Ludwig.

1825 13 October: King Maximilian I Joseph of Bavaria dies. His son Ludwig becomes King of Bavaria as Ludwig I.

15 October: Princess Marie Friederike of Prussia, the mother of Ludwig II, is born as the youngest child of Friedrich Wilhelm of Prussia and his wife Marianne von Hessen-Homburg in Berlin.

1837 24 December: Elisabeth, the later Empress of Austria, is born in Munich as the fourth child of Duke Max and Ludovika in Bavaria.

1842 12 October: Princess Marie of Prussia marries Crown Prince Maximilian of Bavaria in the Church of All Saints in Munich.

1845 7 January: Prince Ludwig, the later King Ludwig III, is born as the eldest son of Prince Luitpold, Maximilian's brother.

25 August: Ludwig II is born as the eldest son of Crown Prince Maximilian and his wife Marie in Nymphenburg Palace (Munich).

26 August: Ludwig is christened Otto Ludwig Friedrich Wilhelm in the Stone Hall of Nymphenburg Palace. His godparents are King Friedrich Wilhelm IV of Prussia and King Otto of Greece (absent).

1848 20 March: March Revolution / Lola Montez scandal. King Ludwig I abdicates in favour of his son Maximilian, whose son Ludwig (II) becomes Crown Prince.

27 April: Birth of Prince Otto Wilhelm Luitpold, the second and last child of Queen Marie and King Maximilian II.

1854 24 April: Emperor Franz Joseph I of Austria marries Duchess Elisabeth in Bavaria (»Sisi«) in Vienna.

2 December: Emperor Franz Joseph I ascends the Austrian throne.

1861 2 February: Crown Prince Ludwig attends a performance of »Lohengrin«, his first Wagner opera, at the Court and National Theatre in Munich.

1862 22 December: Crown Prince Ludwig goes to see the Wagner opera »Tannhäuser« in Munich.

1863 20 September: Crown Prince Ludwig comes of age and swears an oath on the Bavarian Constitution.

1864 Dispute between the German Confederation and the Kingdom of Denmark over Schleswig and Holstein. Austria and Prussia join forces against Denmark.

10 March: Death of Maximilian II. Joseph; his eldest son Ludwig becomes king as Ludwig II.

14 March: Ludwig II's father is buried in the crypt of the Theatine Church in Munich.

27 March: Opening of the *Landtag*, which had been adjourned since 1863. All members of parliament are invited to the royal table. General amnesty for all persons involved in the unrest of 1848/49.

4 May: Ludwig's first meeting with Richard Wagner (audience in the Munich *Residenz*).

1865 10 June: Premiere of Richard Wagner's opera »Tristan and Isolde« in Munich (National Theatre).

27 August: Richard Wagner completes the prose draft of his planned opera »Parsifal«.

18 October: Ludwig attends an unabridged performance of »Wilhelm Tell« by Friedrich Schiller.

20 October to 2 November: Ludwig visits the locations of the William Tell legend in Switzerland.

11 to 18 November: Wagner is the King's guest in Hohenschwangau Castle.

10 December: Following pressure from all sides, the King is forced to ask Wagner to leave Munich. The composer goes into exile in Switzerland (Tribschen near Lucerne).

1866 22 to 24 May: Ludwig II visits Wagner in his Swiss exile on Lake Lucerne.

27 May: Ludwig opens the *Landtag* in person and orders the mobilisation of the Bavarian army against Prussia.

9 June: Prussia invades Holstein and withdraws from the German Confederation.

25/27 June: Ludwig visits the Bavarian troops' main quarters in Bamberg.

June/July: War between Prussia and the German Confederation led by Austria, precipitated by the conflict over Schleswig and Holstein. Bavaria and the Southern German states fight on the side of the Confederation, thus siding with Austria.

3 July: Prussian victory over the Austrians at Königgrätz.

18 August: The North German Confederation is founded under Prussian leadership.

22 August: The Peace of Berlin is concluded. Bavaria is forced to pay war damages and concede border territories to Prussia. Secret alliance of protection and defence between Bavaria and Prussia. In the event of war, the King of Bavaria places his army under the command of the King of Prussia.

10 November to 10 December: Ludwig goes on his first and last journey through his kingdom. He visits the Franconian cities affected by the Austro-Prussian War.

31 December: Prince Chlodwig von Hohenlohe-Schillingsfürst succeeds Ludwig von der Pfordten as President of the Ministerial Council.

1867 22 January: Ludwig becomes betrothed to his second cousin, Duchess Sophie, the daughter of Duke Max in Bavaria and his wife Ludovika, Ludwig I's half-sister.

31 May to 2 June: Ludwig visits Wartburg Castle with his brother Otto.

20 to 29 July: Ludwig visits the World Exhibition in Paris. Conversations with Napoleon III. Due to nationalist sentiment, Ludwig rejects a Southern German alliance with France. Ludwig visits reconstructed Pierrefonds Palace.

26 July: Ludwig's uncle King Otto I of Greece dies in Bamberg. Ludwig breaks off his stay in Paris in order to attend the funeral in Munich.

10 October: Ludwig annuls his betrothal with Sophie.

1868 29 February: Ludwig I dies in Nice.

21 June: Premiere of the »Mastersingers of Nuremberg« by Richard Wagner in the Court and National Theatre in Munich.

2 to 10 August: Ludwig follows his brother to Bad Kissingen and meets the Russian Czar and Czarina.

26 to 28 September: The Russian Czarina is Ludwig's guest in Berg Castle on Lake Starnberg.

First plans for Neuschwanstein Castle.

1869 First construction work on the *Königshäuschen* in the Graswang Valley (Linderhof Palace).

Ludwig asserts himself against the *Landtag*.

Even though the election results are unfavourable for the Ministry, he refuses to dismiss the government, only appointing a new Minister of Culture to replace his unpopular predecessor. The King takes a non-party position.

August: The construction of the King's House on the Schachen mountain begins.

Summer: The refurbishment of Ludwig's apartment in the Munich *Residenz* is completed.

5 September: The foundation stone for Neuschwanstein Castle is laid.

22 September: Premiere of the opera »Rhinegold« in Munich against the will of Richard Wagner.

1870 17 January: The new *Landtag* is opened. Ludwig swears loyalty to the alliance with Prussia.

7 March: Prime Minister Hohenlohe is forced to resign (Count Bray-Steinburg is appointed as his successor).

26 June: Premiere of the opera »Valkyrie« in Munich – once again against Wagner's will.

15 July: The Ministerial Council asks Ludwig to give mobilisation orders.

16 July: Ludwig, who has been informed of the events in Bad Ems (»Ems Dispatch«), demands that the army be mobilised without first informing Bray.

19 July: France declares war on Prussia. Crown Prince Friedrich of Prussia assumes command of the Bavarian troops.

1 September: Battle of Sedan. The French are beaten by the German forces, including the Bavarian army. Napoleon III is taken prisoner.
30 September: Construction of Linderhof Palace begins.
20 October: Ministers Bray-Steinburg, Lutz and Pranckh, authorised by the King, travel to Versailles.
23 November: Treaties of Versailles. Bavaria joins the new German federation and is granted concessions and special rules within the federation.
30 November: Ludwig writes the »Kaiser letter«, in which he offers King Wilhelm I of Prussia the Imperial Crown in the name of all German princes.

1871 18 January: King Wilhelm I is proclaimed German Kaiser in the Hall of Mirrors in Versailles Palace near Paris. Ludwig is represented by his brother, Prince Otto. Founding of the German Reich.
26 February: Treaty of Versailles between the German Reich and France. As a result, Lorraine and Alsace officially become part of the German Reich.
10 May: Treaty of Frankfurt am Main. Prince Otto's health deteriorates.
16 July: Victory parade of the Bavarian troops in Munich, led by Crown Prince Friedrich Wilhelm of Prussia.
21 August: Friedrich, Duke of Hegnenberg-Dux, becomes President of the Ministerial Council.
15 November: Imperial Chancellor Otto von Bismarck is informed of Prince Otto's mental illness.

1872 19 March: Ludwig buys the Gärtnerplatz Theatre in Munich (founded on 25 August 1864), making it the third court stage.
6 May: First private performance for Ludwig II (208 further performances will follow up to and including 12 May 1885).
22 May: The foundation stone of the Bayreuth *Festspielhaus* is laid.

1873 26 September: Ludwig purchases the *Herreninsel* in Lake Chiemsee.

1874 January: Demolition of the *Königshäuschen* in the Graswang valley, final plans for a palace in Linderhof.
21 to 28 August: Ludwig travels to Paris. He celebrates his birthday on 25 August in Versailles.
2 October: Ludwig visits the *Oktoberfest* for the last time.
12 October: On the anniversary of her wedding with Maximilian II, Ludwig's mother Marie converts to Roman Catholicism.

1875 9 February: Bernhard von Gudden, doctor of psychiatry, writes a medical report on Prince's Otto's mental condition.
May: Prince Otto is taken to Schleißheim Palace, where he remains until 1879.
22 August: The King takes part in the Grand Royal Parade on the Field of Mars in Munich for the last time.
24 to 27 August: Ludwig II's interest in the story of Joan of Arc leads him to travel to Reims.

1876 The Cabinet Treasury is threatened with bankruptcy.
May: Ludwig II buys the »Moorish Kiosk« for the park of Linderhof Palace.
6 to 9 August: Wagner's four-part opera cycle »The Ring of the Nibelung« is premiered in Bayreuth. Ludwig II attends the dress rehearsals.
27 to 31 August: Ludwig attends the third, public »Ring« cycle in Bayreuth.
Construction of »Hunding's Hut« near Linderhof Palace.

1877 The Cabinet Treasury continues to struggle. Ludwig II refuses to curb his building activities.
25 August: Completion of the »Venus Grotto« in the park of Linderhof Palace.
»Gurnemanz's Cell« is constructed close to »Hunding's Hut« following descriptions in the (unfinished) opera »Parsifal« by Richard Wagner.

1878 21 May: The foundation stone for Herrenchiemsee Palace is laid.

1880 Minister of Culture Johann von Lutz becomes the new President of the Ministerial Council.
13 March: Prince Otto is taken from Schleißheim to Fürstenried Palace, as his mental condition has deteriorated further. He remains in this palace until his death on 11 October 1916.
22 August: The King's last proclamation to the Bavarian people.
Bavaria celebrates 700 years of the House of Wittelsbach as rulers of Bavaria.

1881 13 March: Czar Alexander II is killed in St Petersburg in a bomb attack. Ludwig II's fear of assassination increases.
27 June to 14 July: Ludwig travels to Switzerland with the actor Josef Kainz.
29 September to 7 October: Ludwig stays on the *Herreninsel* and in Herrenchiemsee Palace.

1882 26 July: Premiere of »Parsifal« in Bayreuth.

1883 13 February: Richard Wagner dies in Venice.
Plans to build a castle on the Falkenstein mountain near Pfronten in the Allgäu.

1884 16 May: Ludwig purchases the ruined Falkenstein Castle.
27 May to 8 June: Ludwig stays in the royal apartment in the palas of Neuschwanstein Castle for the first time.
Ludwig takes out a bank loan of 7.5 million marks to continue building his castles.

1885 Ludwig's debts climb to around 14 million marks.
The King refuses to stop building. The entire ministry and Prince Luitpold attempt to bring order into Ludwig's finances.
15 October: Queen Mother Marie and Ludwig meet for the last time to mark her birthday. Ludwig shows his mother Neuschwanstein Castle.
Autumn: Construction work on Herrenchiemsee Palace is discontinued.

1886 January: Ludwig II has plans drawn up for a summer palace in the style of a Chinese palace.

23 March: The psychiatrist Dr Bernhard von Gudden declares his willingness to produce a medical evaluation diagnosing the King as insane.

5 May: The Ministerial Council's request that the King should come to Munich to start sorting out his finances goes unheeded.

8 June: A medical evaluation created at the request of Minister Lutz declares Ludwig II to be suffering from advanced mental illness. A committee is set up to inform the King of his removal from office and take him into custody.

10 June: Prince Luitpold is proclaimed Prince Regent. First unsuccessful attempt by the committee to arrest the King in Neuschwanstein Castle.

12 June: At a quarter to one in the morning, Dr von Gudden and some wardens manage to arrest Ludwig. At four o'clock in the morning, the deposed King departs for Berg Castle on Lake Starnberg, where he arrives at twelve thirty.

13 June: Shortly before seven in the evening, von Gudden and Ludwig set out on a walk in the park of Berg Castle. At eleven at night, the bodies of the two men are found floating in Lake Starnberg.

19 June: Ludwig's body is buried in the crypt of St Michael's Church in Munich, mourned by the people.

1 August: The King's castles (Herrenchiemsee, Linderhof and Neuschwanstein) are opened to the public.

16 August: Following Wittelsbach tradition, the King's heart is placed in a urn in the Shrine of Our Lady in Altötting.

Picture credits

Hessian State Archives Darmstadt, shelfmark D 27 A No. 18/6: 22

Austrian National Library Vienna, shelfmark Pf 1124:B (10): 73

Collection Jean Louis Schlim, Munich: 34, 49, 85

Collection Marcus Spangenberg, Regensburg: 10, 17, 38, 41, 57, 61, 97, 107, 121, 122, 129, 130, 135, 141, 143, 157, 164, 166

Cover images: Front cover: Portrait of Ludwig II. of Bavaria around 1870. – Photograph; back cover: Posterity saw Ludwig II the way he wished to see himself: as Lohengrin, knight by the grace of God. – Coloured postcard, 1899 (both images: collection Marcus Spangenberg)

Bibliography

Baumgartner, Georg: Königliche Träume. Ludwig II. und seine Bauten, Munich 1981.

Böhm, Gottfried: Ludwig II. König von Bayern. Sein Leben und seine Zeit, Berlin ²1924.

Botzenhart, Christof: »Ein Schattenkönig ohne Macht will ich nicht sein.« Die Regierungstätigkeit König Ludwigs II. von Bayern (Schriftenreihe zur bayerischen Landesgeschichte, ed. Kommission für bayerische Landesgeschichte bei der Bayerischen Akademie der Wissenschaften Vol. 142), Munich 2004.

Evers, Hans Gerhard: Ludwig II. von Bayern. Theaterfürst – König – Bauherr. Gedanken zum Selbstverständnis, ed. J. A. Schmoll gen. Eisenwerth, revised by Klaus Eggert, Munich 1986.

Gebhardt, Heinz: König Ludwig II. und seine verbrannte Braut. Unveröffentlichte Liebesbriefe Prinzessin Sophie's an Edgar Hanfstaengl, Pfaffenhofen 1986.

Haasen, Gisela: Ludwig II. Briefe an seine Erzieherin, Munich 1995.

Hacker, Rupert (ed.): Ludwig II. von Bayern in Augenzeugenberichten, Düsseldorf 1966.

Hacker, Rupert: König Ludwig II., der Kaiserbrief und die »Bismarck'schen Gelder«. In: Zeitschrift für bayerische Landesgeschichte 65/3 (2002), p. 911–990.

Hierneis, Theodor: Der König speist. Erinnerungen aus der Hofküche König Ludwigs II., Munich 1953.

Hommel, Kurt: Die Separatvorstellungen vor König Ludwig II. von Bayern. Schauspiel, Oper, Ballett, Munich 1963.

Hüttl, Ludwig: Ludwig II. König von Bayern. Eine Biographie, Munich 1986.

Kobell, Louise von: König Ludwig II. von Bayern und die Kunst, Munich 1900.

Merta, Franz: »Gottes Licht auf Erden zu verkünden.« Das Herrscherethos König Ludwigs II. von Bayern und die Entstehung des König-Ludwig-Kults. In: Zeitschrift für bayerische Landesgeschichte 56/3 (1993), p. 725–768.

Petzet, Michael und Bunz, Achim: Gebaute Träume. Die Schlösser Ludwigs II. von Bayern, Munich 1995.

Praxmarer, Mario und Adam, Peter: König Ludwig II. in der Bergeinsamkeit von Bayern und Tirol. Bergresidenzen – Schlösser – Begegnungen – Krise – Mysteriöser Tod, Garmisch-Partenkirchen 2002.

Prinz von Bayern, Adalbert: Erinnerungen 1900–1956, Munich 1991.

Rauch, Alexander: Schloss Herrenchiemsee, Munich 1995.

Reichold, Klaus: Keinen Kuß mehr! Reinheit! Königtum! Ludwig II. von Bayern (1845–1886) und die Homosexualität, Munich 2001.

Schad, Martha: Bayerns Königinnen, Regensburg ³1995.

Schlim, Jean Louis: Ludwig II. – Traum und Technik, Munich ²2010.

Schmid, Alois und Weigand, Katharina (eds.): Die Herrscher Bayerns. 25 historische Portraits von Tassilo III. bis Ludwig III., Munich ²2006.

Spangenberg, Marcus: The Throne Room in Schloss Neuschwanstein. Ludwig II of Bavaria and his vision of Divine Right, Regensburg 1999.
Strobel, Otto (ed.): König Ludwig II. und Richard Wagner. Briefwechsel in 5 Bänden, Karlsruhe 1936–1939.

Selected websites

www.schloesser.bayern.de
The official homepage of the Bavarian Administration of State-owned Palaces, Gardens and Lakes, which is in charge of Herrenchiemsee, Linderhof, the Munich *Residenz*, Neuschwanstein and the King's House in Schachen.

www.hohenschwangau.de
Official homepage of the administration of Hohenschwangau Castle for the objects in possession of the Wittelsbach equalising fund endowment (including Hohenschwangau Castle and Schlosshotel Lisl), with offers for shopping and overnight stays (package deals!).
The site also contains a link to the ticket centre in Hohenschwangau that sells tickets for Hohenschwangau and Neuschwanstein Castles.

www.ludwig2bayern.de
Currently the most up-to-date information portal on King Ludwig II of Bavaria. It contains mainly press articles that can be accessed worldwide, ordered according to keywords.

www.koenig-ludwig.org
Extensive bibliography and registers of persons.

www.koenig-ludwig-chronik.de
Biographical account of the life of Ludwig II, illustrated throughout with contemporary newspaper and magazine illustrations (wood engravings).

www.marcusspangenberg.de
On his homepage, the author of this book presents information on past and current lectures, publications, cultural trips and events about Ludwig II.

Bibliografische Information der Deutschen Nationalbibliothek
Die Deutsche Nationalbibliothek verzeichnet diese Publikation in der Deutschen Nationalbibliografie; detaillierte bibliografische Angaben sind im Internet über http://dnb.d-nb.de abrufbar.

ISBN 978-3-7917-2744-8

English translation: Margaret Hiley, Oakham, Rutland
Design (cover and text): Martin Veicht, Regensburg
Typesetting: Vollnhals Fotosatz, Neustadt a. d. Donau
Printing and binding: Friedrich Pustet, Regensburg
Printed in Germany 2015

Other publications from our catalogue can be found at www.verlag-pustet.de
Contact and orders via verlag@pustet.de